PHANTS TRUNK (DRUNK) DONE LIKE A DOG

ROT **HAV** ... WIL

CHOOKS ... **KIC**

ENT **RU** ... **D FL**

LIKE A BULL AT A GATE **COCK AND BUL**

BOUT A DOG DEAD AS A DODO **STONE TH**

E BEES KNEES NERVOUS AS A MOTHER ROO I

ORSE AND CHASE THE RIDER I'M AS DRY AS

A DOG (GET DRINKS ON CREDIT) **ELEPHANT**

AWAY WITH THE BIRDS PISSED AS A PARRO

LIKE THE BOTTOM OF A COCKY'S CAGE **M**

THE CHOOK HOUSE DOWN FLY IN TH

FLY WITHIN A BULL'S ROAR **STARVE TH**

SOMETHING THE CAT DRAGGED IN **SEE A MA**

OWS KNEE HIGH TO A GRASSHOPPER **JUST TH**

ROOM FULL OF PICKPOCKETS **I COULD EAT**

AMEL DRIVER'S BUM **GALAH (FOOL)** TO TIE U

RUNK (DRUNK) DONE LIKE A DOGS DINNE

PARROT **HAVE A HAIR OF THE DO**

Australianimal

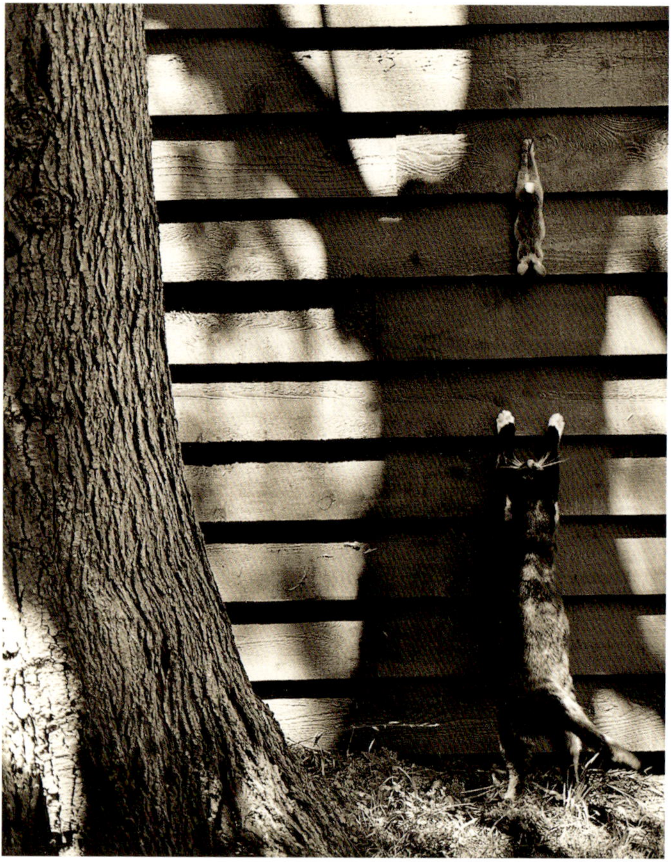

Arcadia

THE BUDGIE SMUGGLERS GUIDE TO

Australian Animals

PHOTOGRAPHED AND WRITTEN BY

Robert Billington. AUSTRALIA

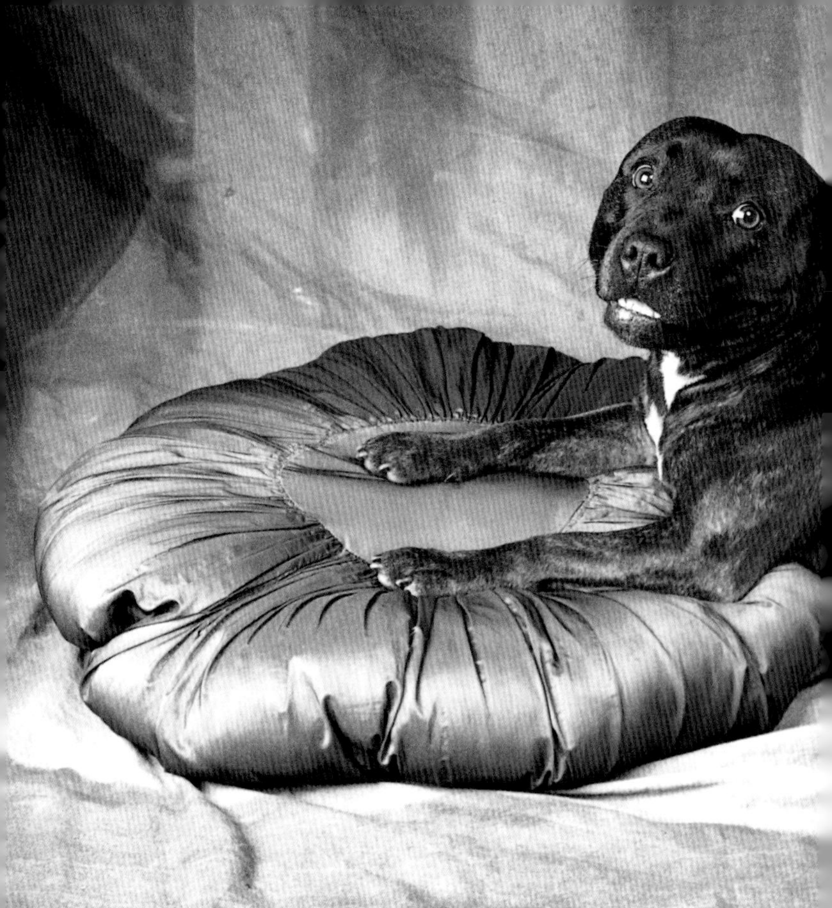

LOOK AT ME, LOOK AT ME!
Crows Nest

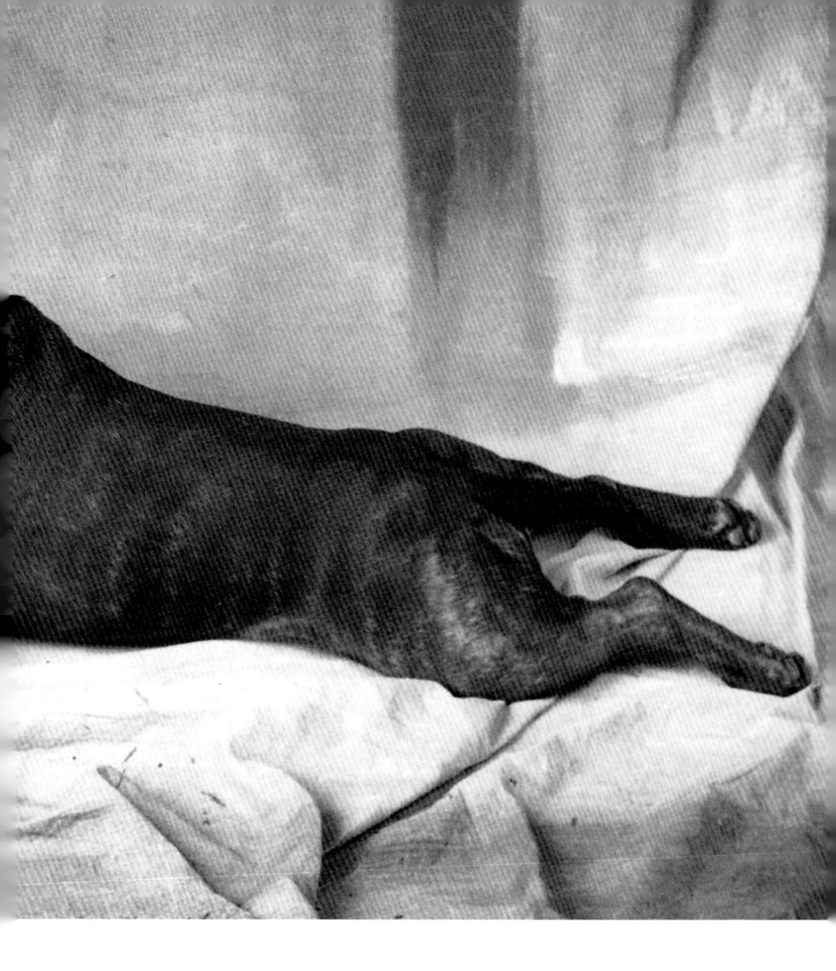

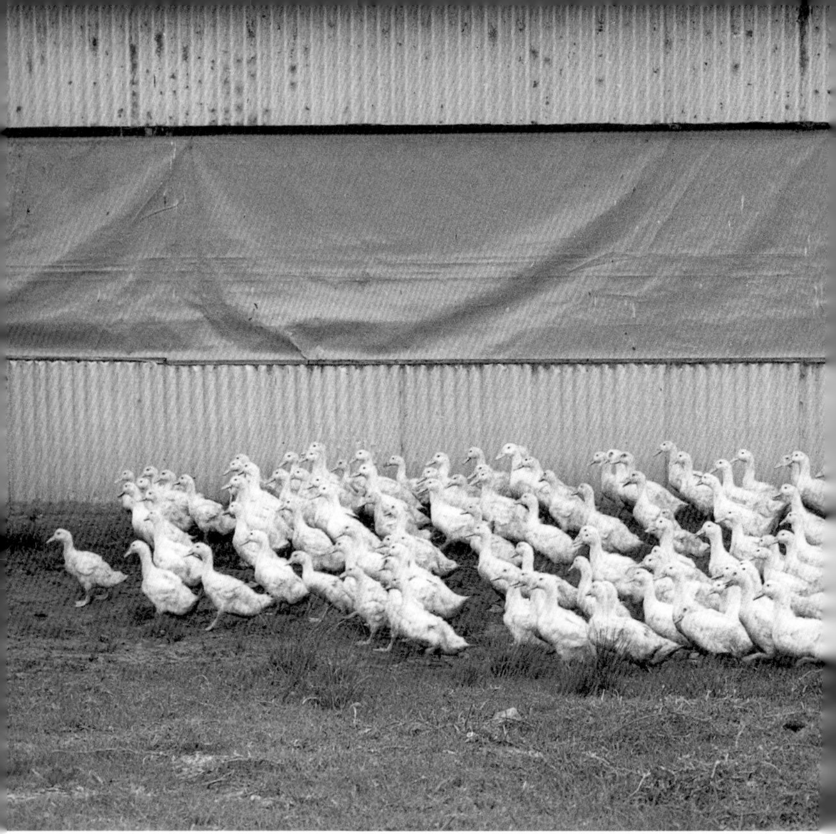

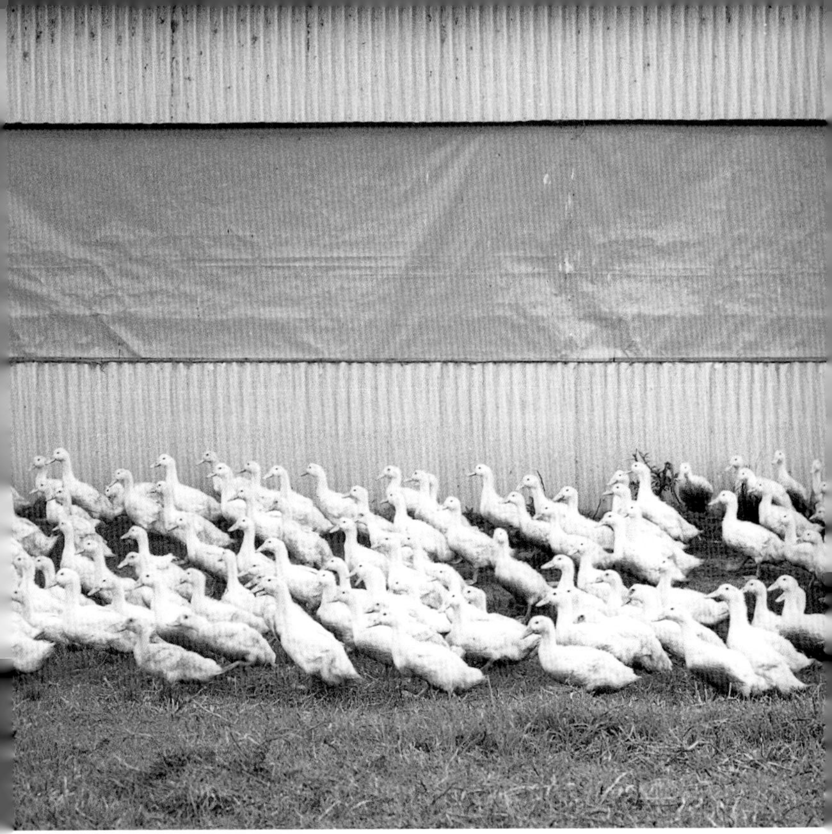

QUACK TROOPS
Arcadia

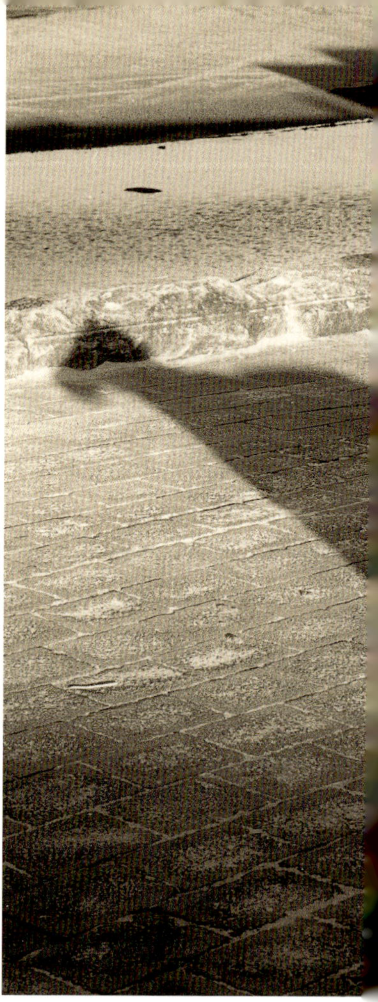

HOW LONG IS A DOGS SHADOW?
Queenscliff

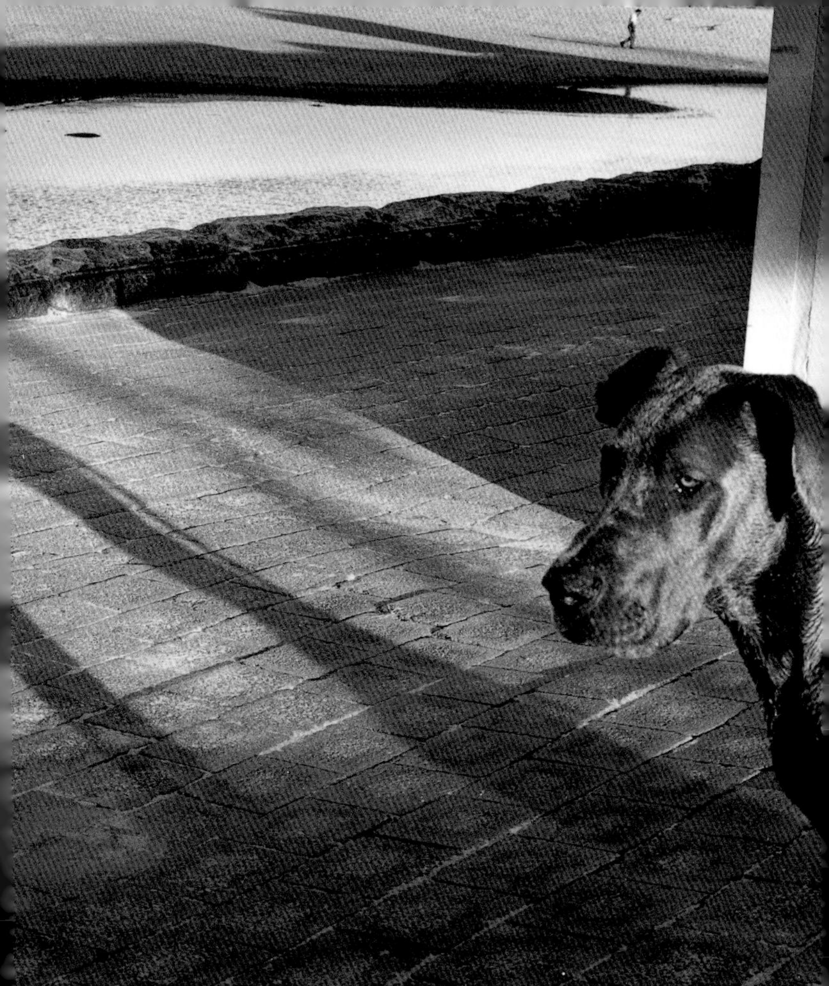

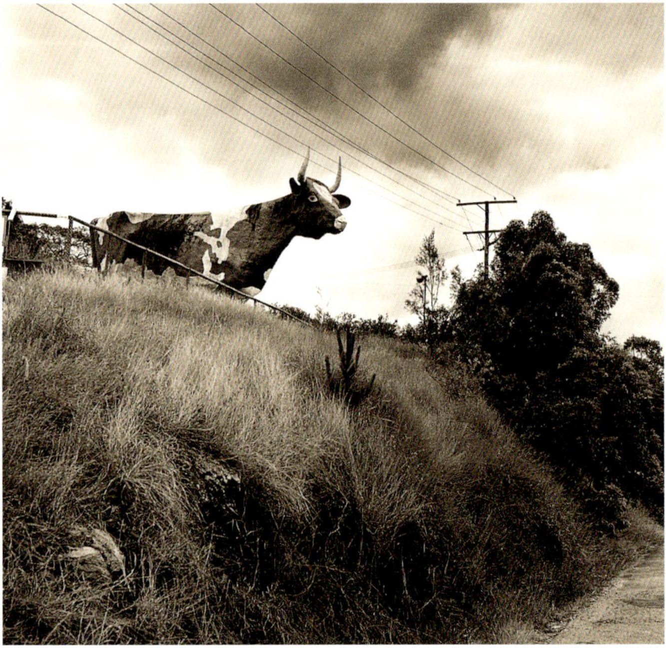

Australianimal

The dictionary definitions of the terms 'Australian' and 'Animals' inspired me to coin my own word specifically for the purposes of this book.

"Australianimal: a collection of fair-dinkum photographs of any living thing that is not plant or mineral; generally being feather or fur or hide covered and capable of voluntary motion and sensation, etc."

I've always carried a camera, waiting to capture that elusive moment when a cat decides to stretch and yawn or a camel rests its head flat on the ground. Photographs are golden opportunities realised, mysterious accidents distilled to a split second. A joey on Observatory Hill, how did that happen? Or the shot of an old man taking great pleasure in feeding magpies, all patiently waiting their turn. In Batemans Bay I couldn't believe my luck when I saw twenty seagulls lined up at an invisible starter's gun, while on the opposite railing five pelicans aired their own wings and views. Further inland at the Canberra Show, a man in a black suit and bowler hat ran past just as a horse paralleled his stride. Man and horse merged. Click!

The two camels at Sydney's Balmoral Beach? They were being taken to a Christmas party by an Arabic gentleman. More luck. And when was the last time lions leapt through burning hoops at an Australian circus? I can't remember, but I had the kids and camera in tow to capture the moment. Driving through the outback, camera at the ready, I saw a massive flock of sparrows, waiting to swoop down and devour the wheat spilt from passing trucks. Scenes straight out of Hitchcock's film 'The Birds'. Not one, but two flocks of pigeons flying in unison, dart and cluster like a swarm of bees, then suddenly disperse into threatening clouds above Orange as thunder roared and lightning clapped.

I went through a period of inviting people to my studio with their pets — everything from French Poodles and Borzois to a Dingo who hid under the backdrop for 20 minutes before agreeing to one photograph. The camouflaged dog blended obligingly into his background then broke into song. The three dogs on the steps, sitting for a formal portrait, wouldn't take things seriously until I barked orders at them. Gentle suggestion often helps — for example, persuading three men to dress as sharks and pose for me at Bronte Baths, or asking a farmer "would you mind walking your Alpacas across the Sydney Harbour Bridge?" Mind you, the 141 white ducks waddled to the right shed with little persuasion from me. Click! Thanks, lads.

My actor friend needed publicity photographs surrounded by an audience. "Why not use ducks?" I suggested. And so we did. Let's face it, animals enhance any scene. I met an architect who kept a goat in his office and a pig carrying the sign 'A tidy home is the sign of a dull woman'. A vet rang to ask "could you come and photograph my duck?" And yes, there is a gorilla emerging from a very ordinary building in Goulburn and a Dalmatian who will smile on request.

The white rhino peering from the shrubbery is, in fact, freshly made from plaster of Paris, ready to be transported to Dubbo Zoo. And the fifteen Alpacas, very much alive, look buried waist deep. "That's just how they sit." "And why don't they sit in the shade?" I asked. "Because in Peru, the cougars and large cats perch in trees, pounce on the Alpacas and eat them." "Oh."

An elephant approaches. Is that the Taj Mahal in the background? No it's an Indian restaurant sign on the road to Byron Bay. Nothing's quite what it seems, including that ink blot which is really two horses after their hose-down. The greyhound race at Moss Vale had no punters at all, an absence clearly arranged by the rabbit. I wandered into the hairdresser's in Yass to find a stuffed rooster sitting on two golden eggs staring intently across the street at a sheep munching on a lamington. It's true!

Meanwhile, the donkey dreams of wilder days and a solitary emu eyes my camera. Could I take your picture? Would you mind? Click. Keep still. Thanks. Click. A parade of animals letting me into their world, obeying not my requests, but their own private musings. Photographing Australianimals — as mysterious and imaginary as the secret art of cat herding.

Robert Billington

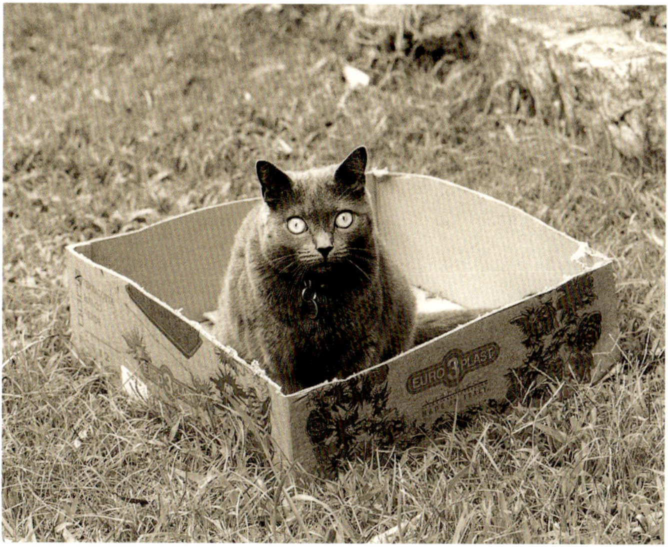

I'M SURE THERE'S MEANT
TO BE LITTER IN HERE

TO TIE UP A DOG (GET DRINKS ON CREDIT) **ELEPHANTS TRUNK (DRUNK)** DONE LIKE A DOGS DINNER **AWAY WITH THE BIRDS** PISSED AS A PARROT **HAVE A HAIR OF THE DOG** MOUTH WILL FEEL LIKE THE BOTTOM OF A COCKY'S CAGE **MY CHOOKS TURNED INTO ROOSTERS AND KICK THE CHOOK HOUSE DOWN** FLY IN THE OINTMENT **RUN AROUND LIKE A BLUE ARSED FLY** WITHIN A BULL'S ROAR **STARVE THE LIZARDS** LIKE A BULL AT A GATE **COCK AND BULL** SOMETHING THE CAT DRAGGED IN **SEE A MAN ABOUT A DOG** DEAD AS A DODO **STONE THE CROWS** KNEE HIGH TO A GRASSHOPPER **JUST THE BEES KNEES** NERVOUS AS A MOTHER ROO IN A ROOM FULL OF PICKPOCKETS

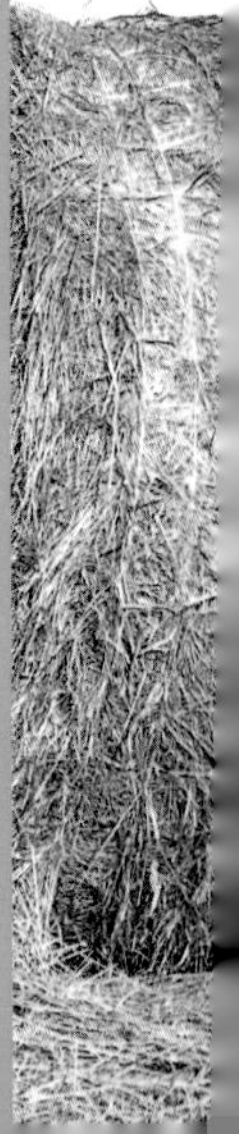

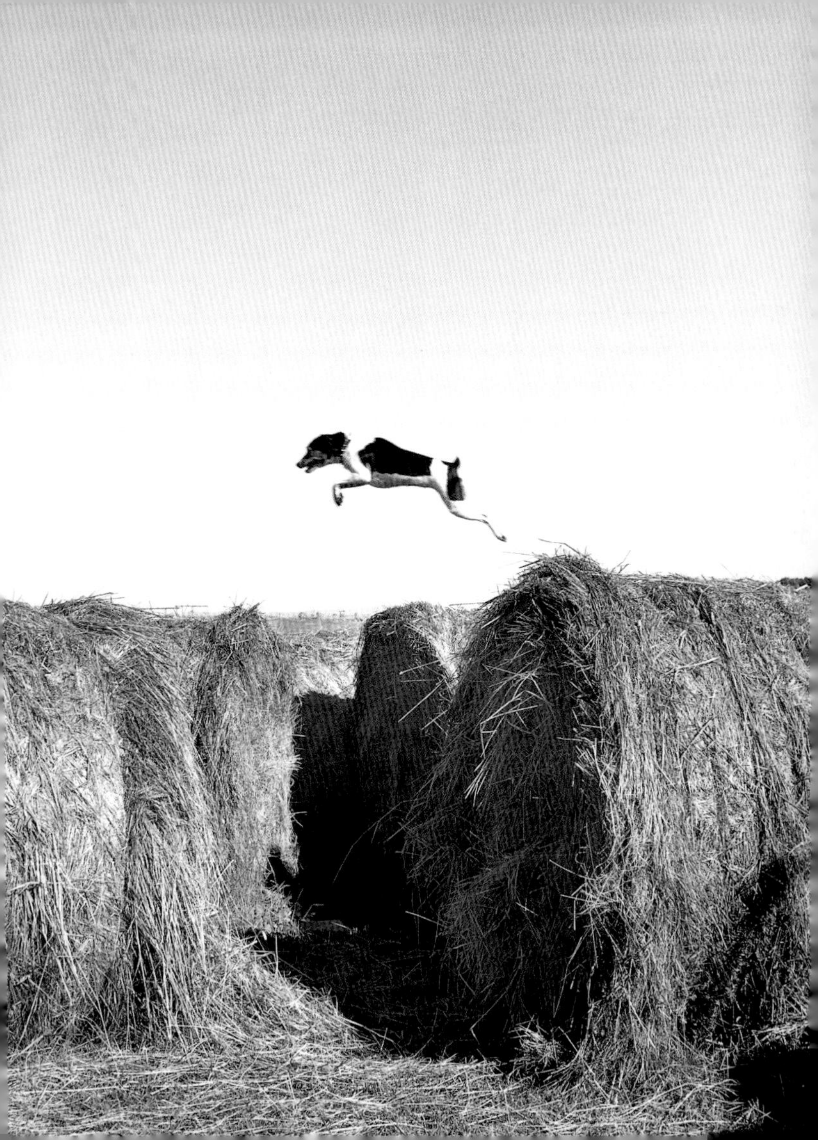

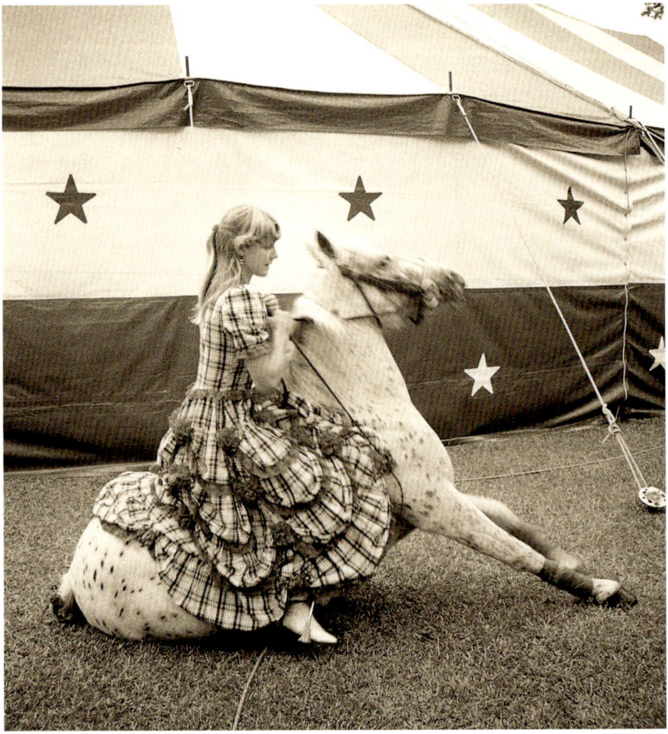

SPARKLEHORSE
St Ives

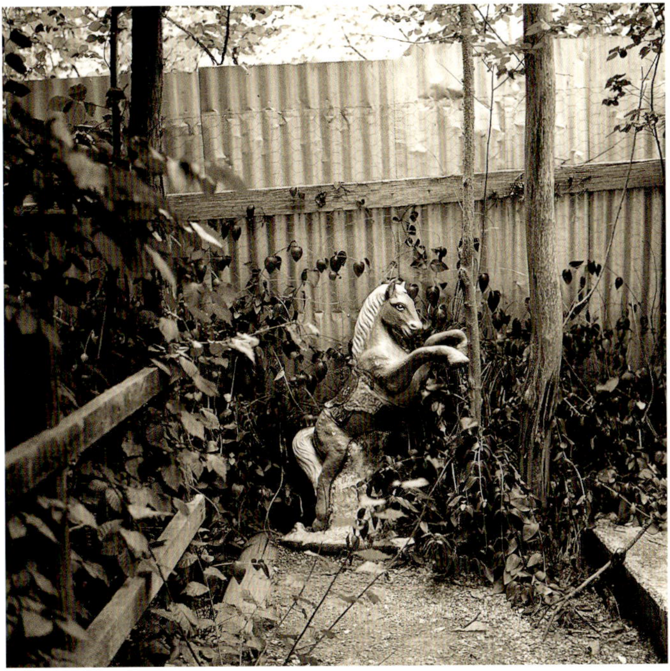

Maldon

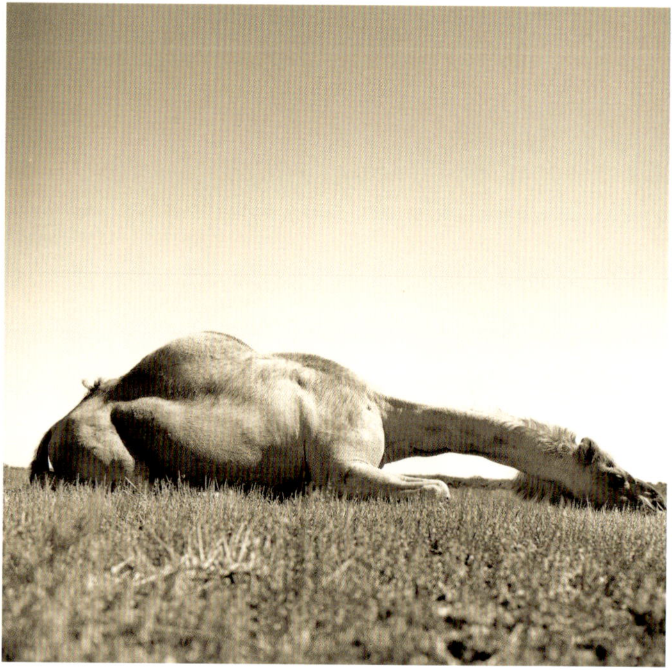

A MAN'S NOT A CAMEL ...

The Rocks, Sydney

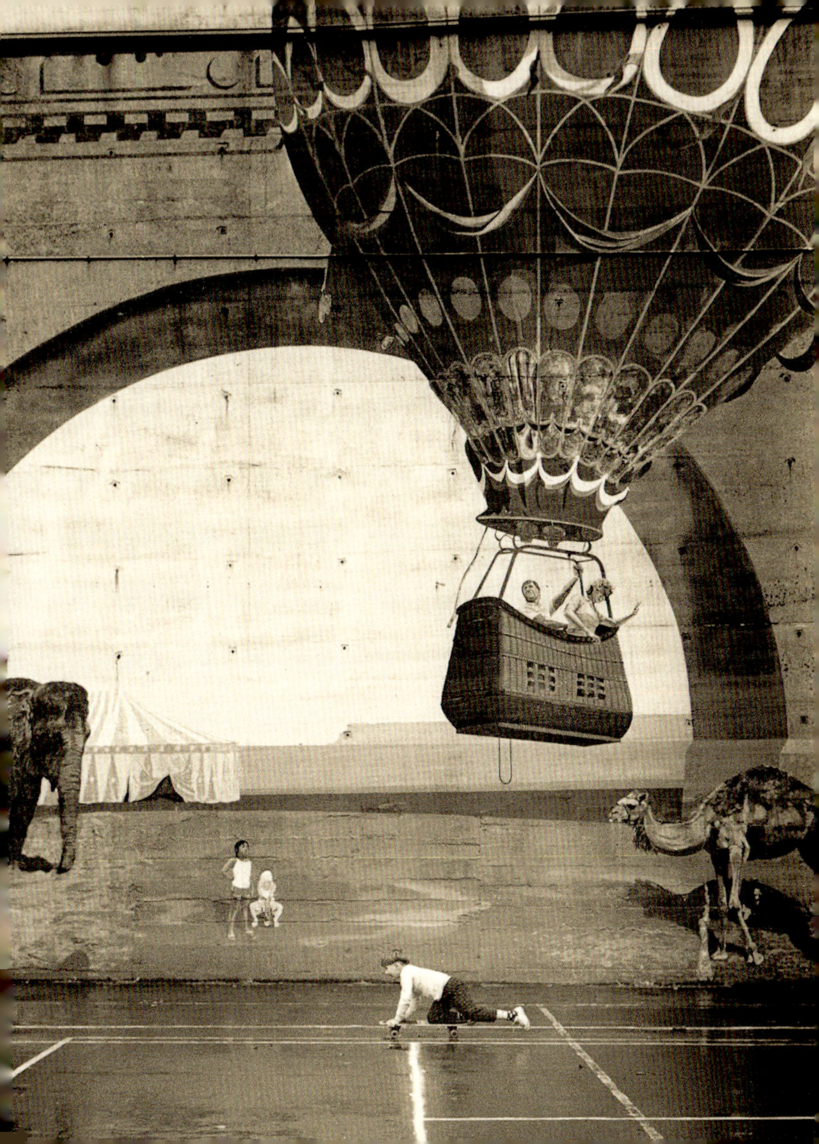

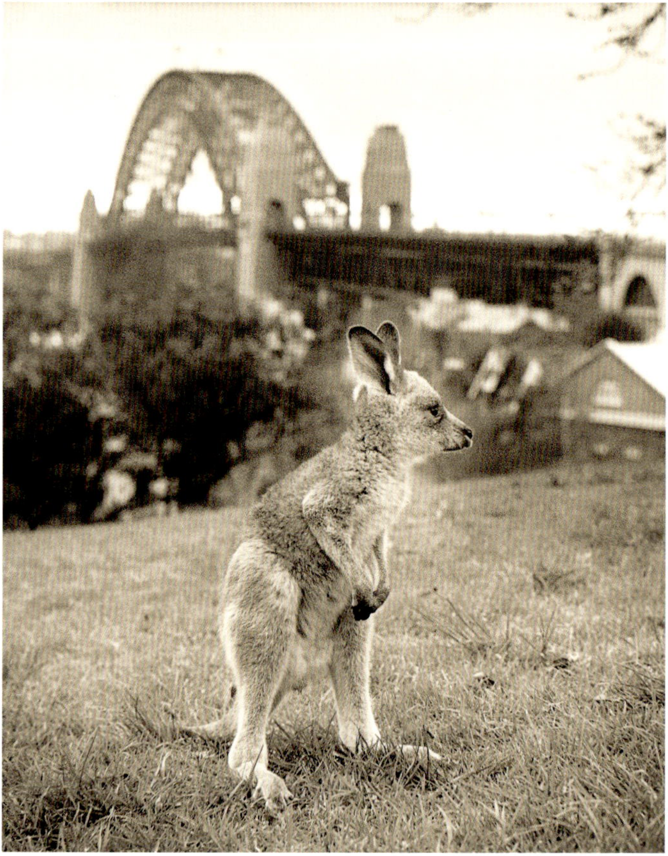

A FEW ROOS LOOSE IN THE TOP PADDOCK
Observatory Hill, Sydney

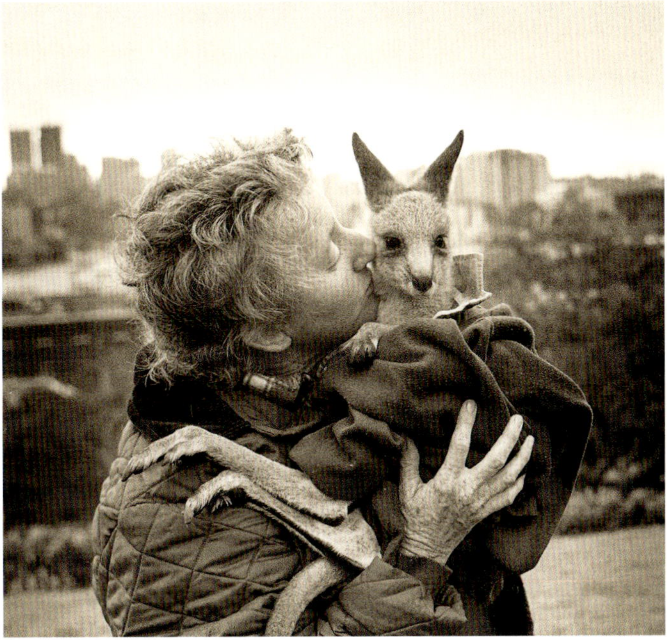

Joey Hopper

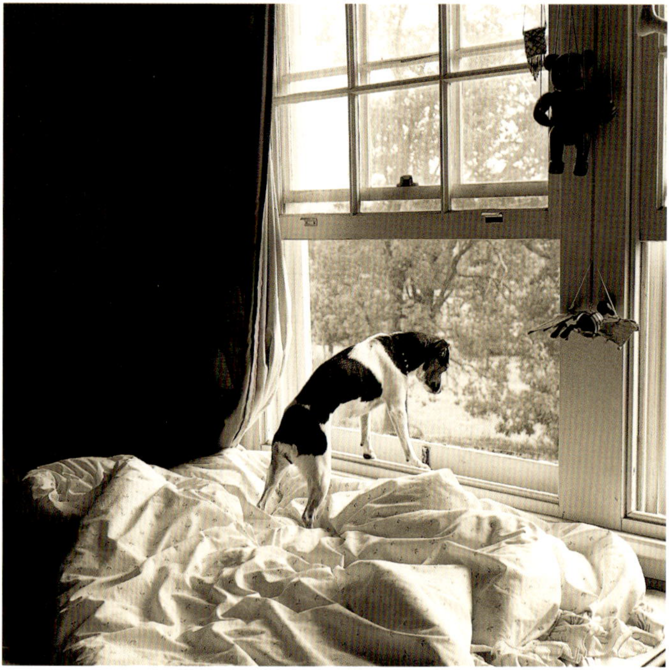

OGLE
Yass

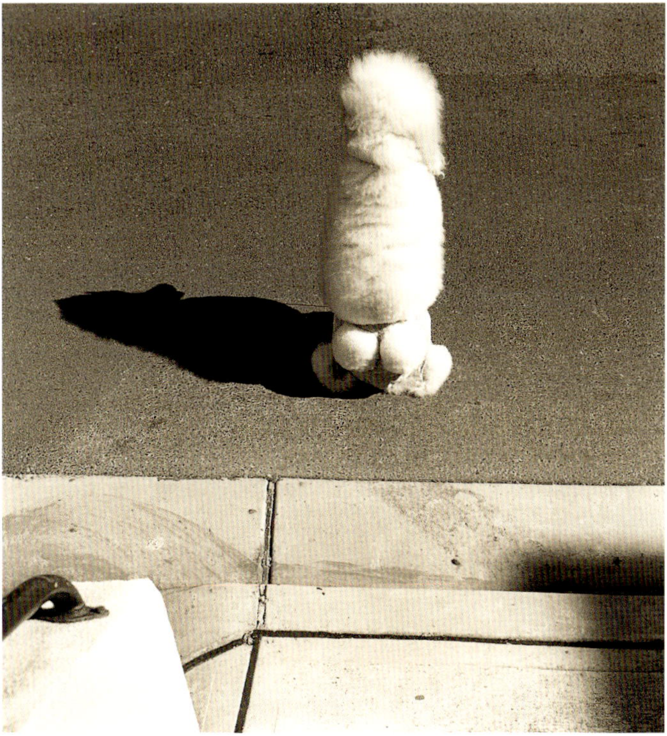

Crows Nest, Sydney

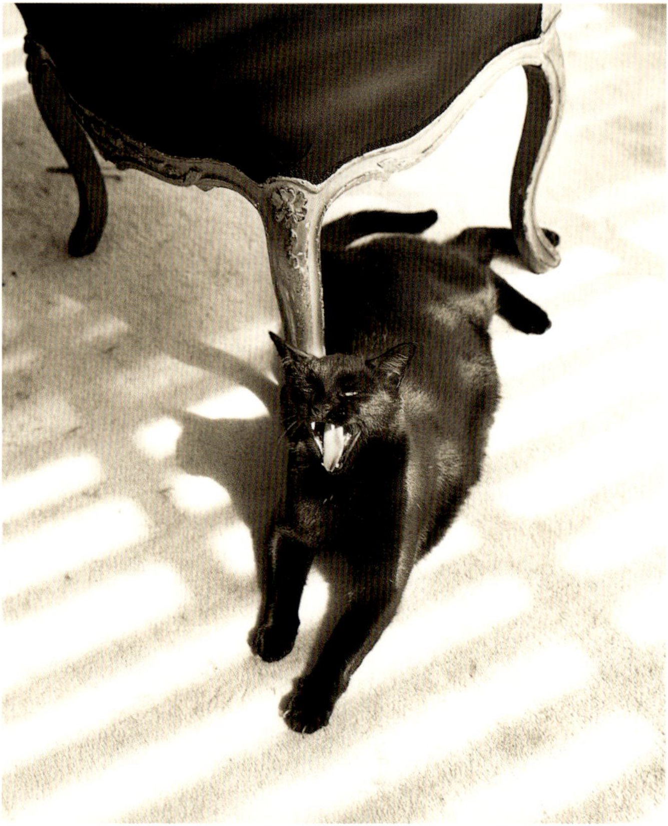

YACKETY-YAK, YABBER, YAWN?
Double Bay

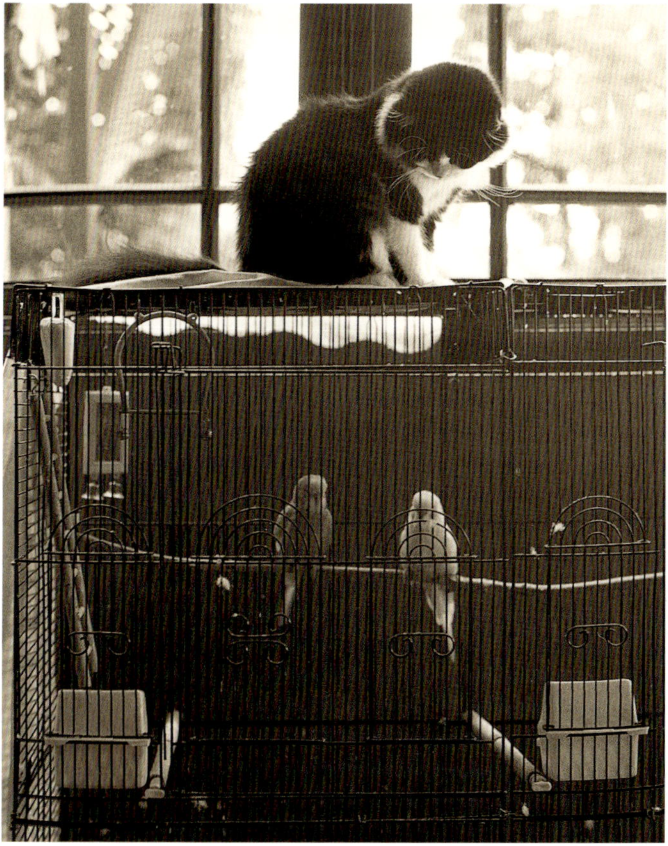

YUM!

Two, four, six, eight,
Bog in, don't wait
Knives and forks
As sharp as razors,
Fill your bellies,
And go like blazes!

Crows Nest

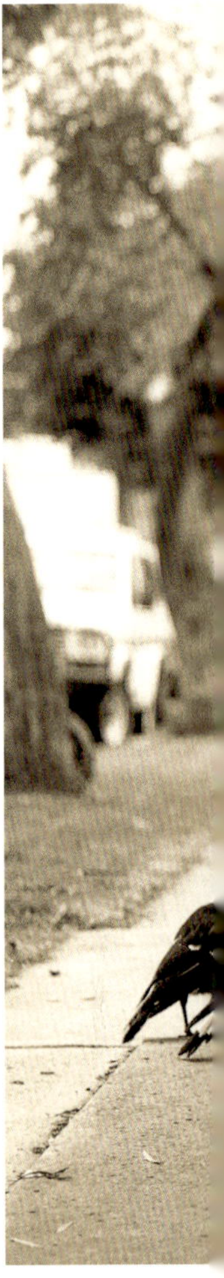

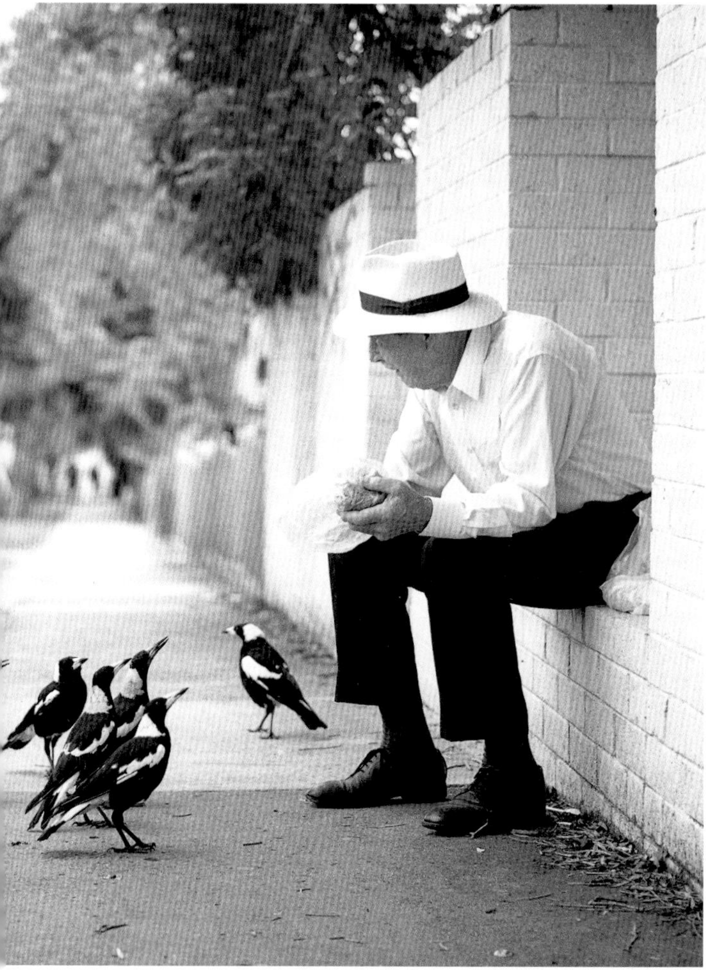

YOU CAN LEAD A HORSE TO WATER ...

Hunter Valley

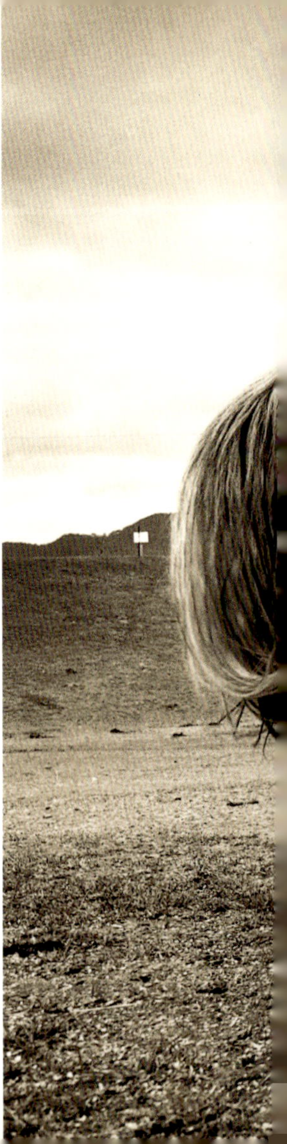

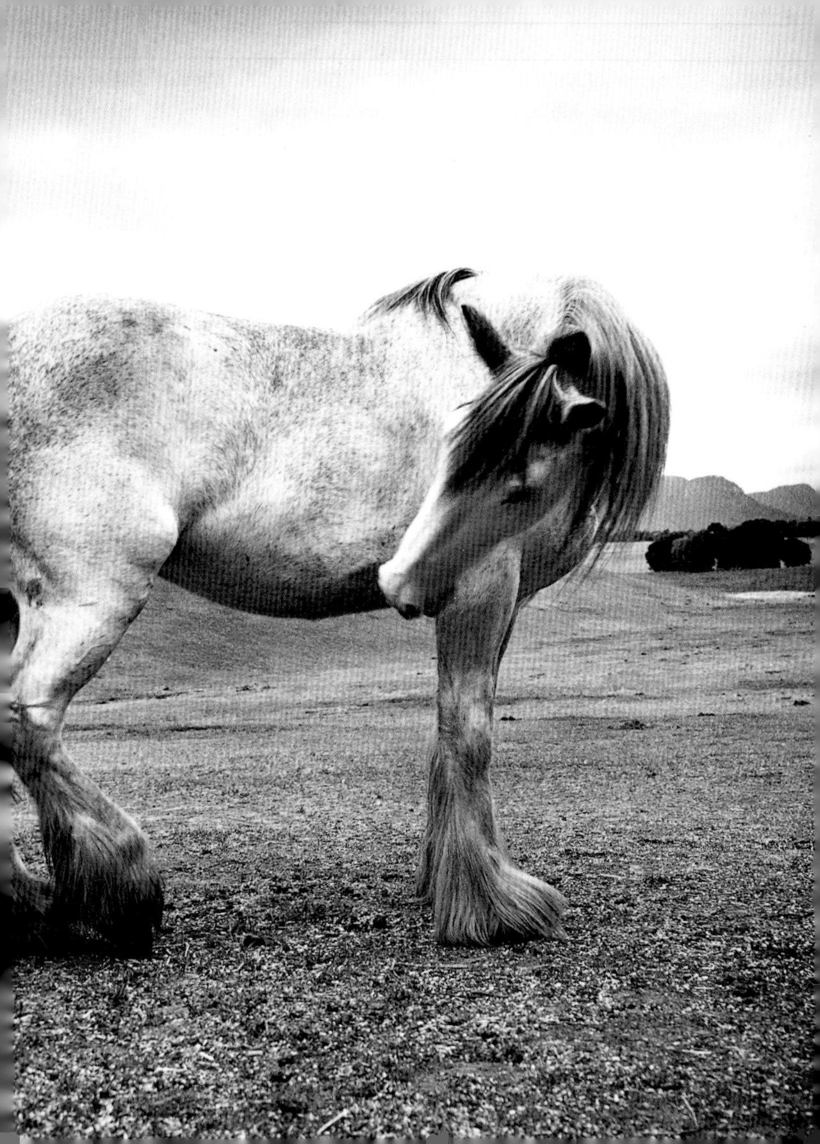

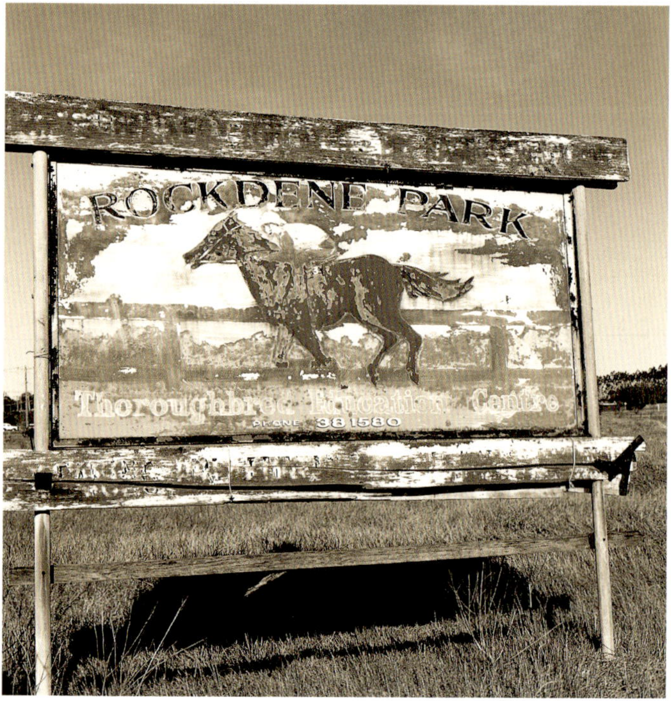

Hunter Valley

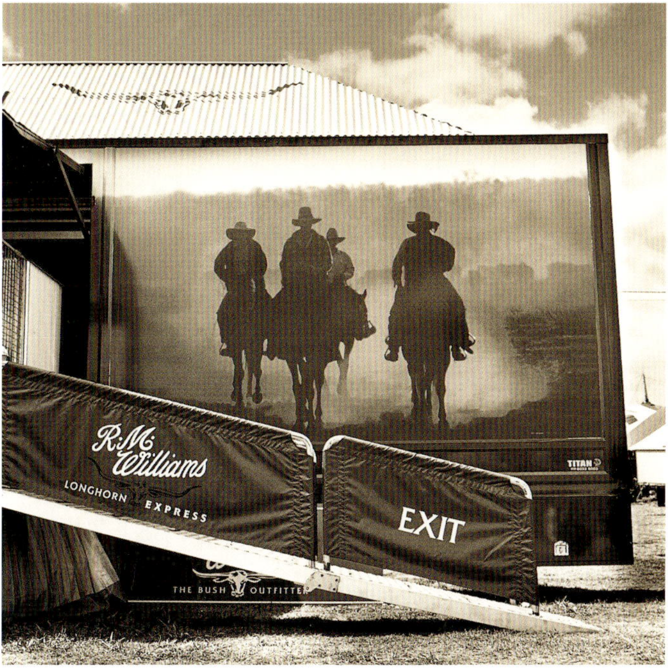

R.M. WILLIAMS PASSED AWAY NOVEMBER 2003
Canberra

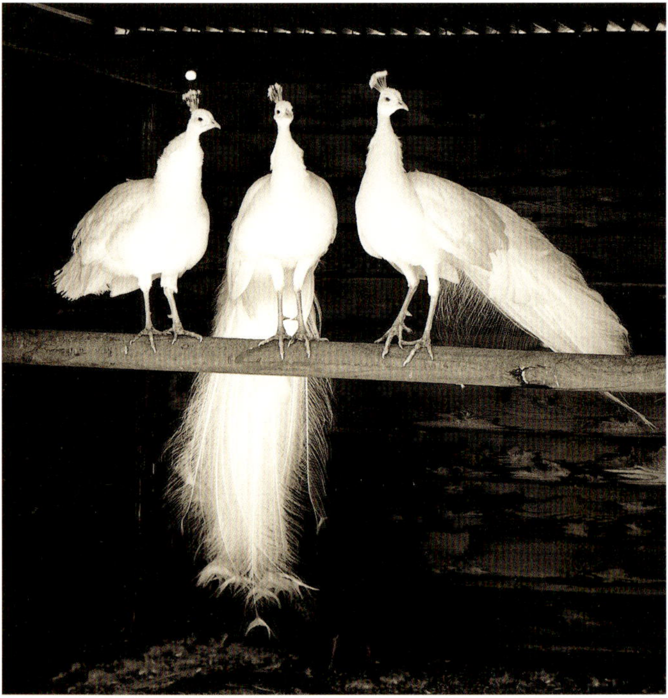

PROUD AS A PEACOCK
Yass

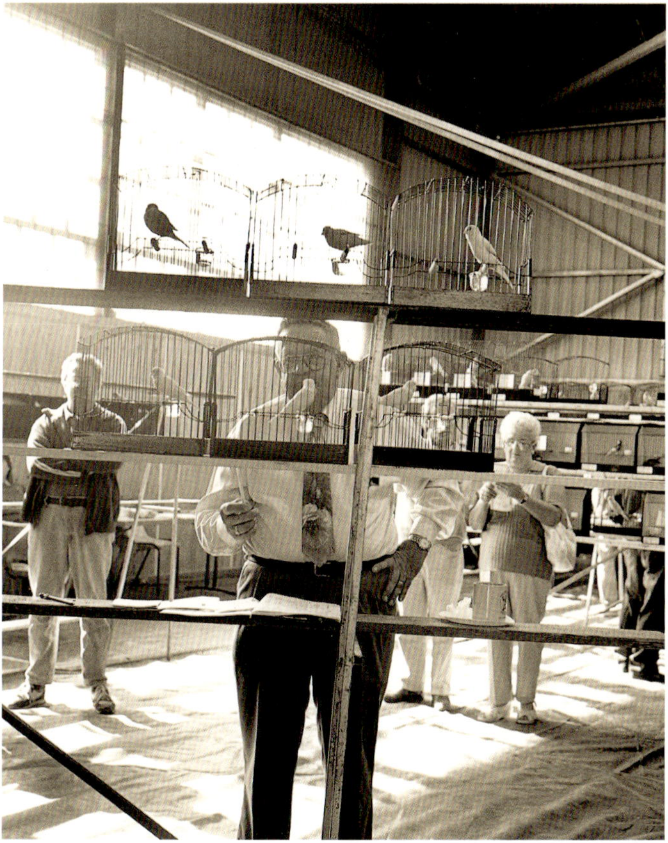

WATCH THE BIRDIE
Yass Bird Show

SITTING ON
THE FENCE
Batemans Bay

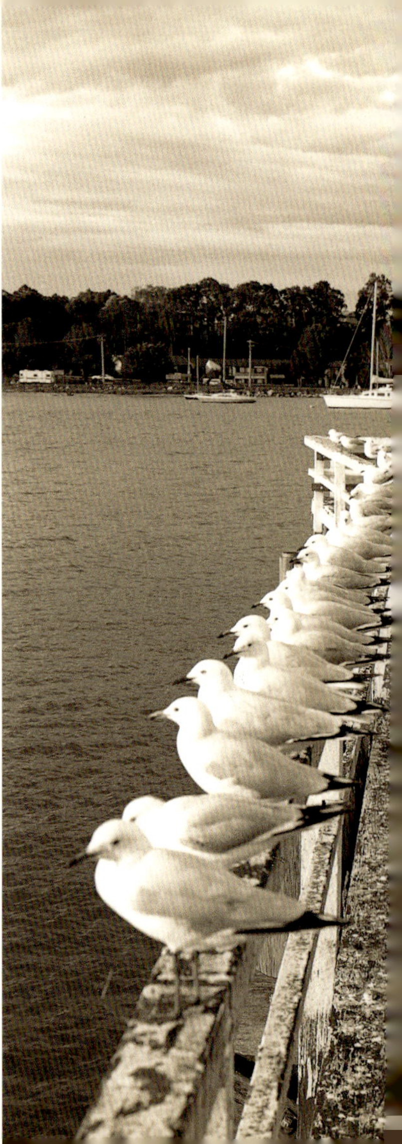

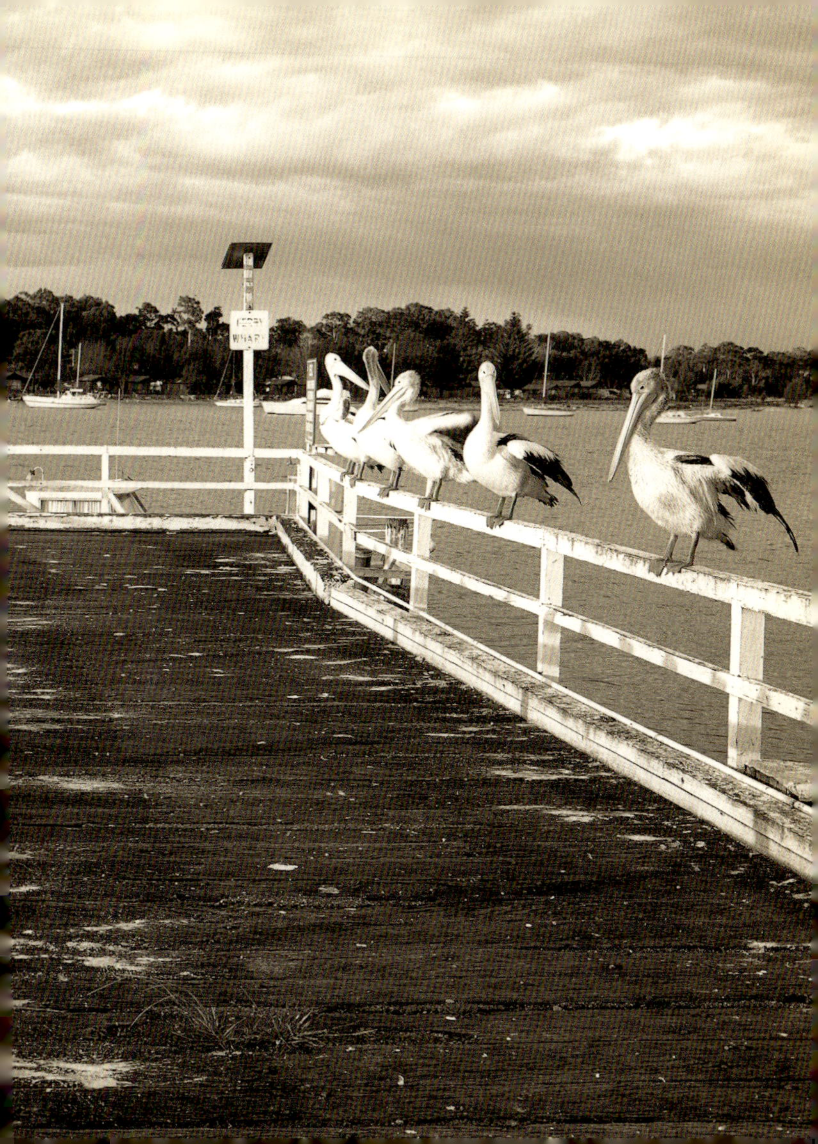

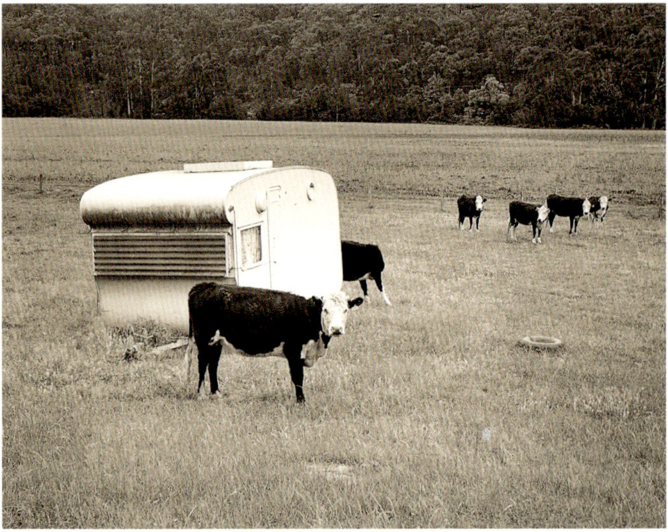

I ASKED — DO THEY HAVE FOXTEL?
Wiseman s Ferry

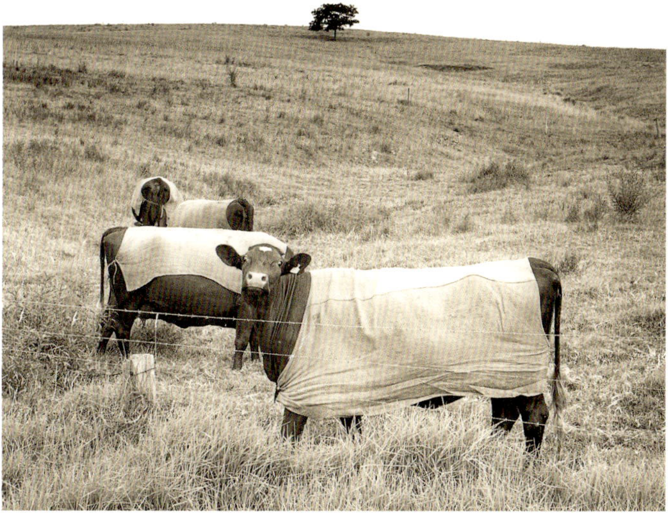

Kangaroo Valley

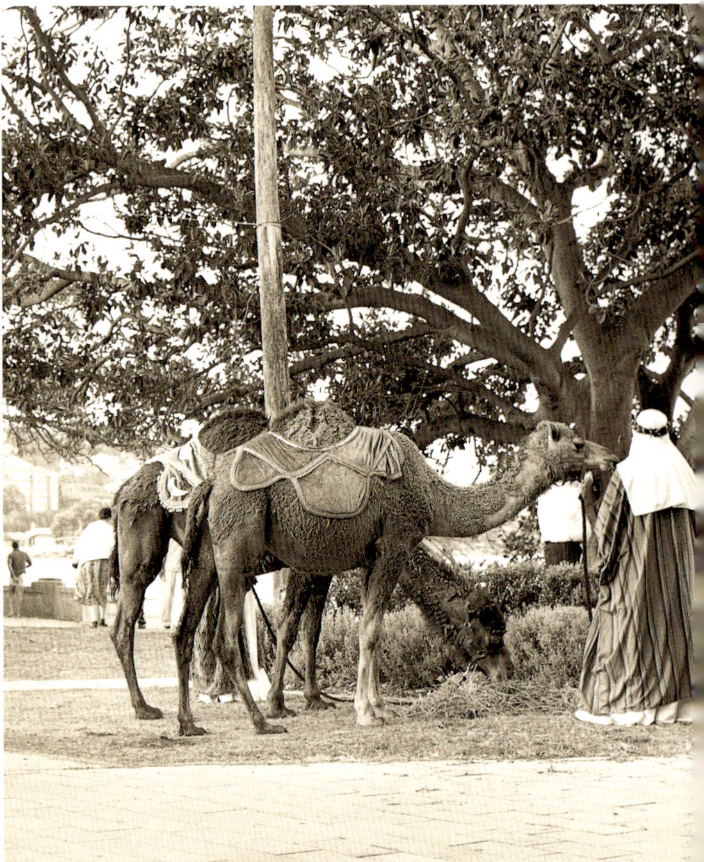

ONE HUMP OR TWO?
Balmoral Beach

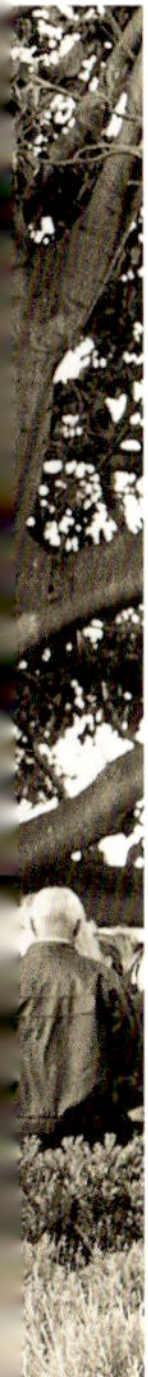

I hope the fleas of a
thousand camels infest
your underwear!

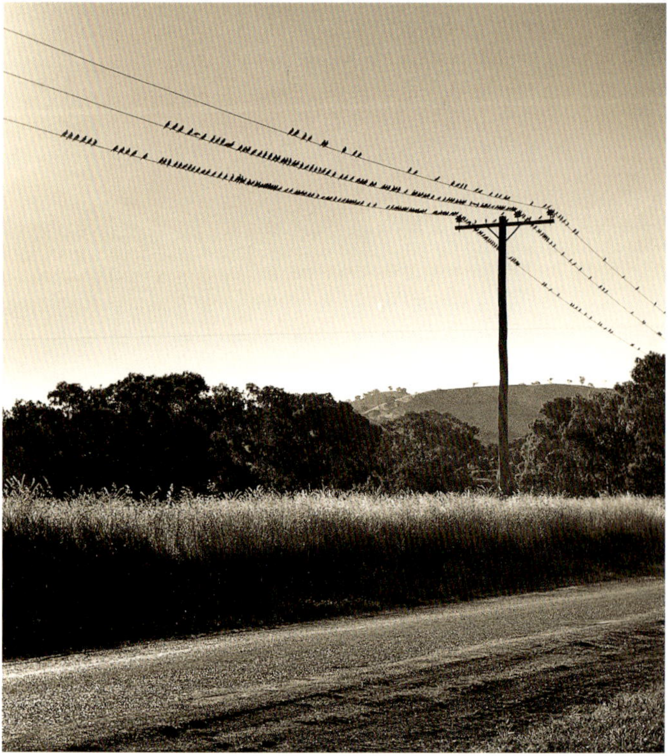

ON THE LINE
Gundagai

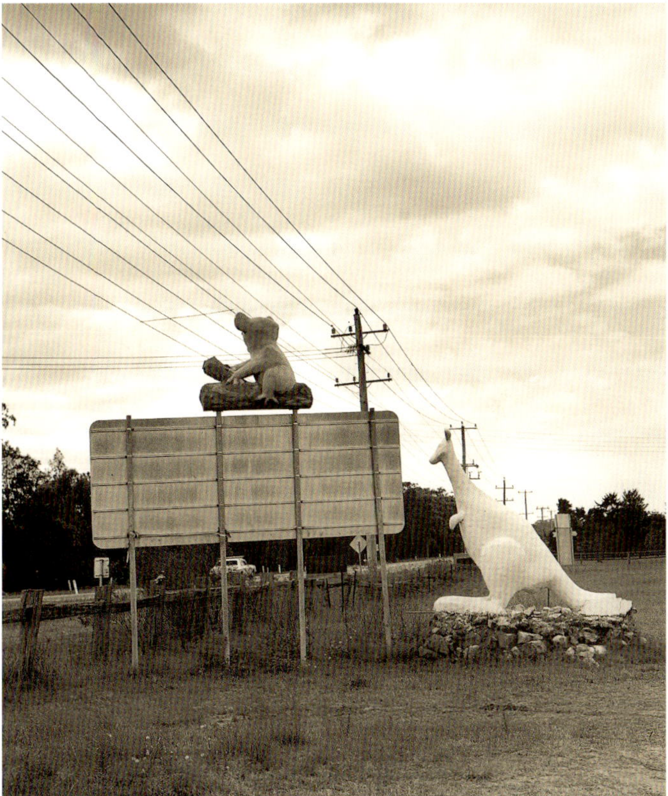

Near Nelson Bay

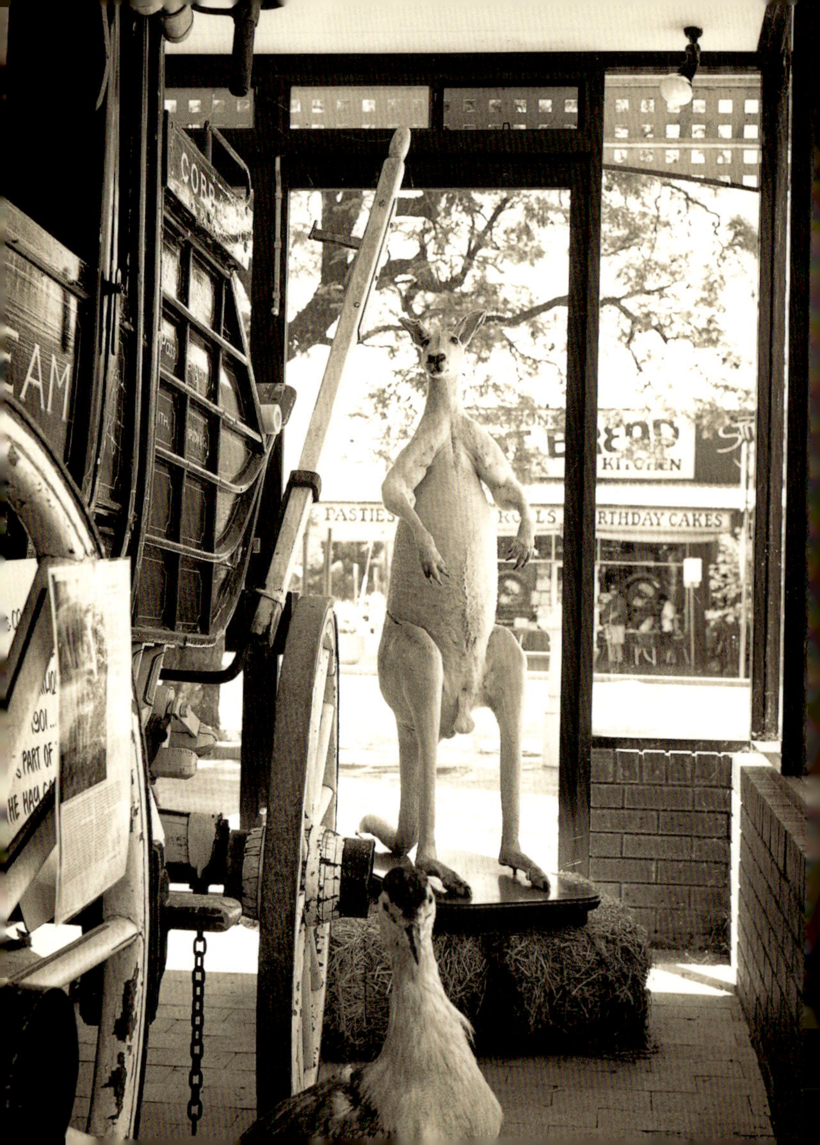
KITCHEN
PASTIES

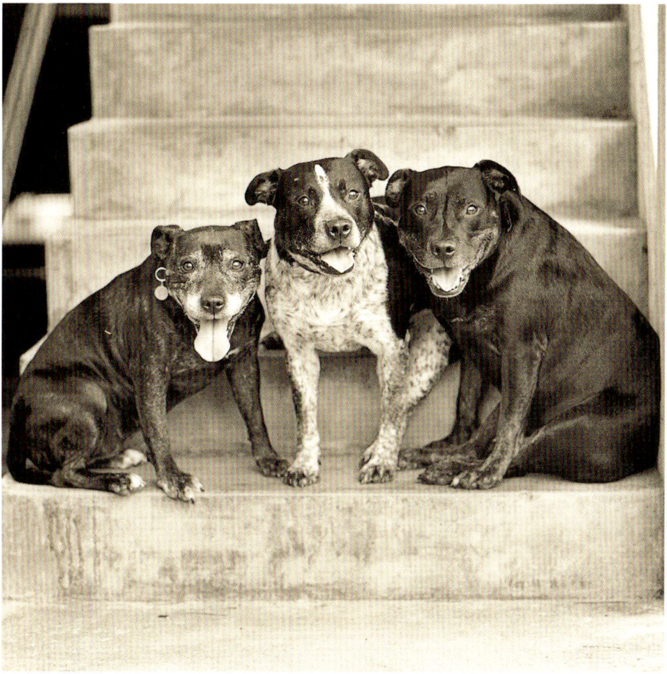

BARKING ATTENDANTS
Crows Nest

WHITE KANGAROO
Hay

Overleaf:
LION TAMER, Collaroy

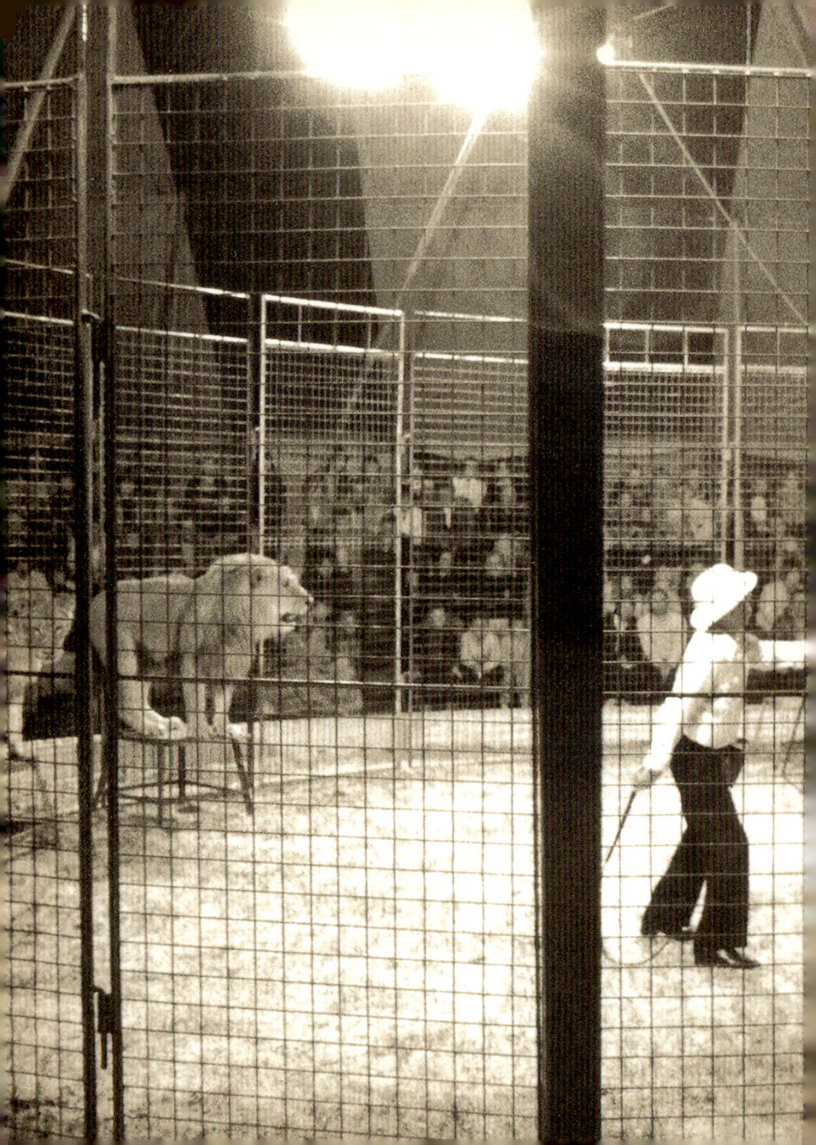

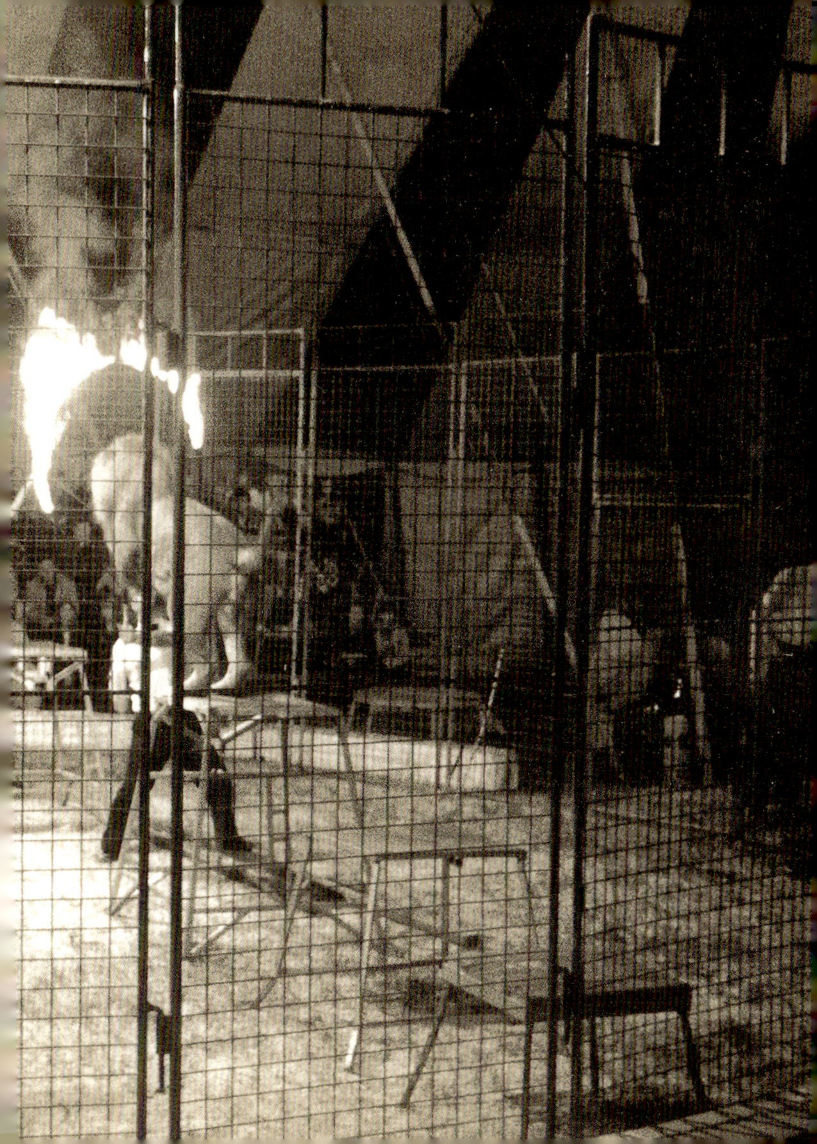

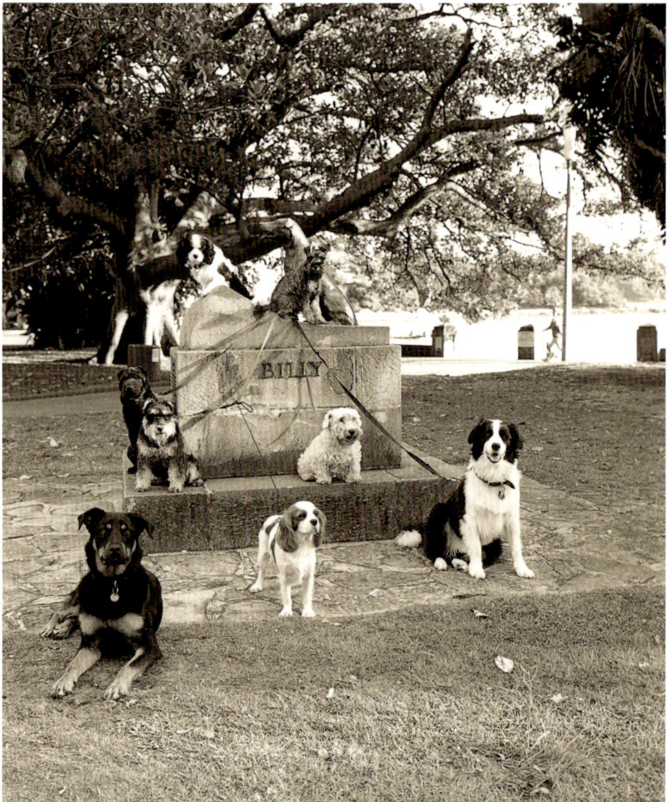

DOG SITTERS
Balmoral

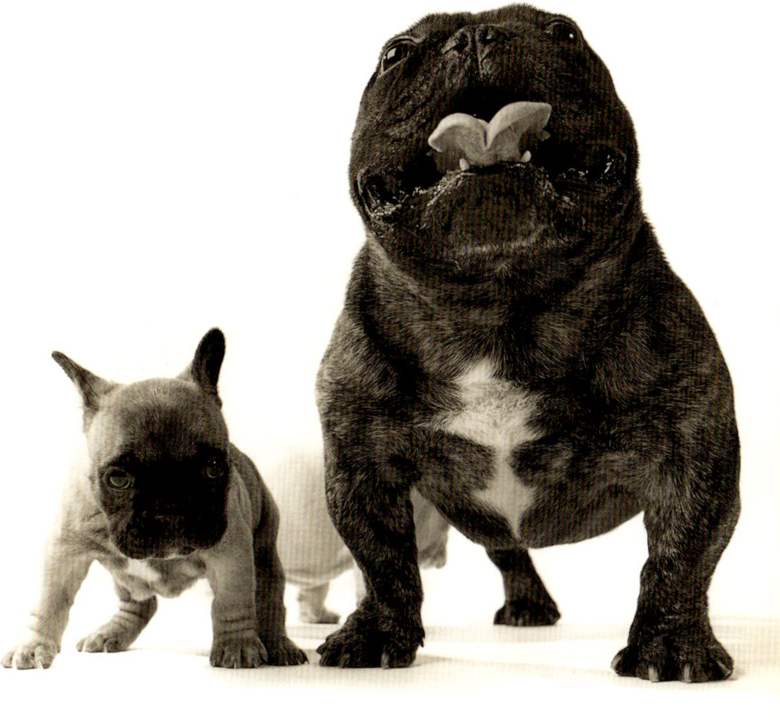

MOTHER AND DAUGHTER
Crows Nest

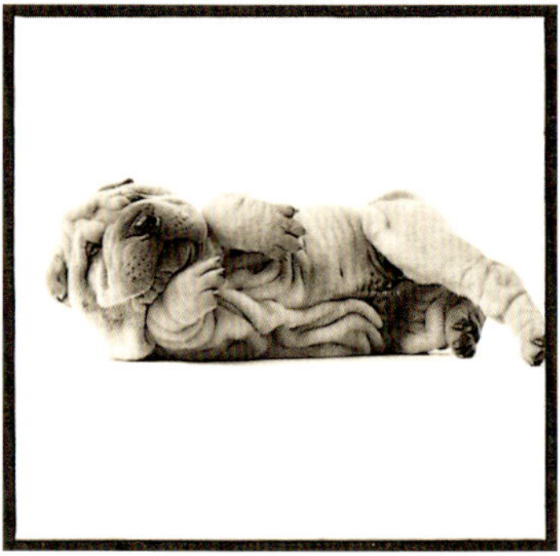

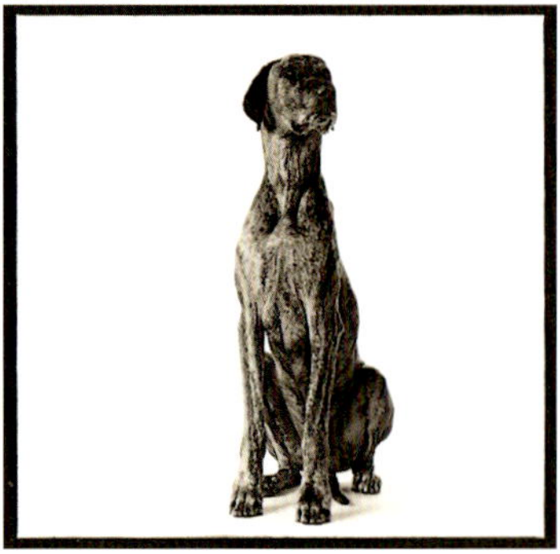

WRINKLY DOG, GREAT DANE

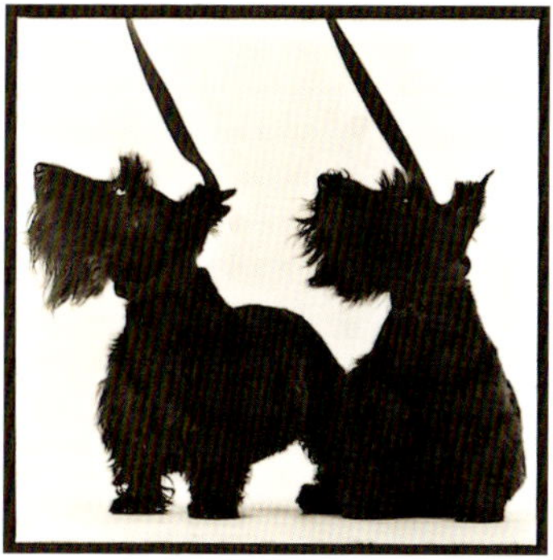 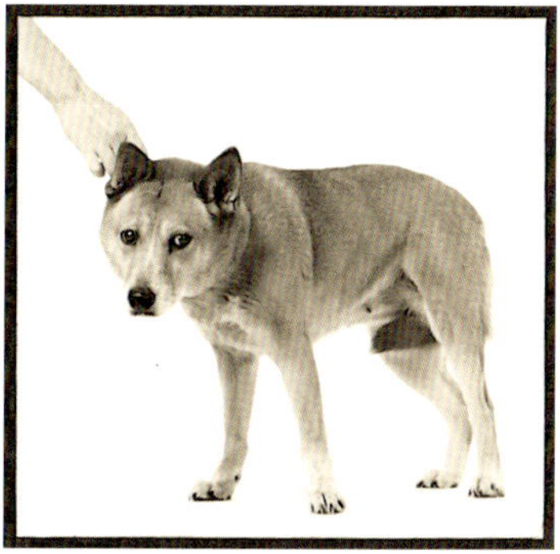

SCOTTIES, DINGO

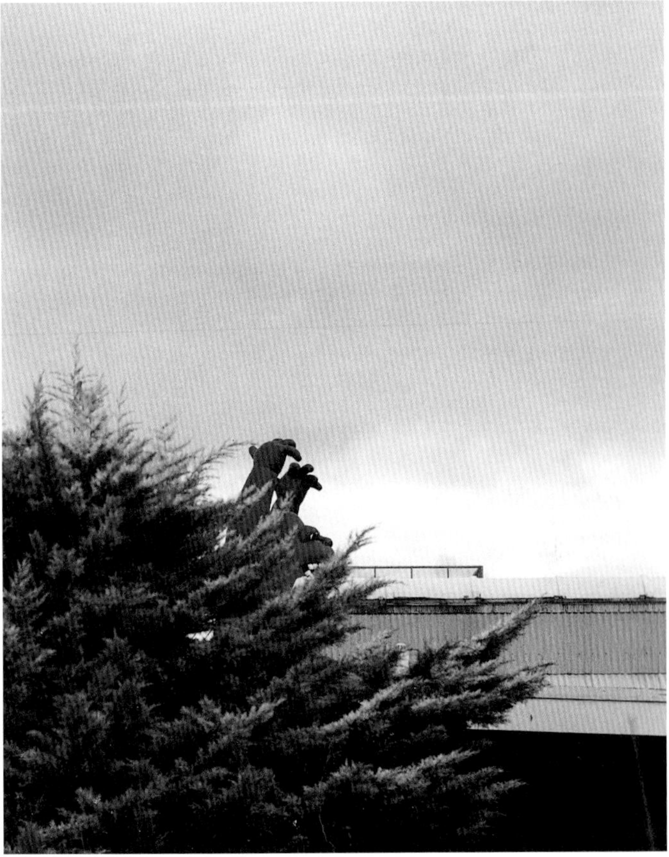

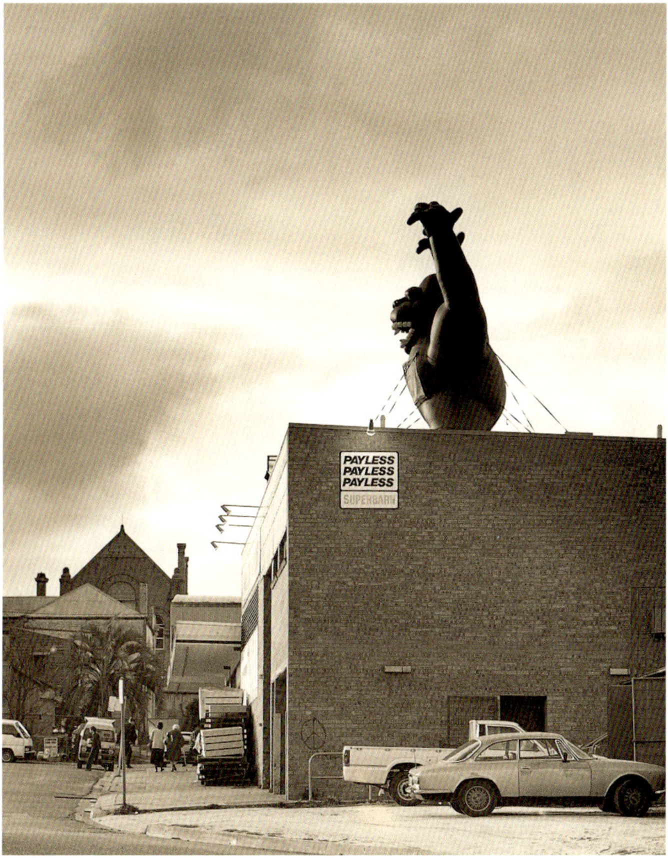

GORILLA GRAM
Goulburn

LOWER THAN A SNAKE'S BELLY
WOULDN'T SHOUT IN A SHARK
ATTACK (HOW MISERABLE CAN YOU
GET) TO TIE UP A DOG (GET DRINKS
ON CREDIT) ELEPHANTS TRUNK
(DRUNK) DRUNK AS A SKUNK AWAY
WITH THE BIRDS PISSED AS A
PARROT HAVE A HAIR OF THE DOG
MOUTH WILL FEEL LIKE THE BOTTOM
OF A COCKY'S CAGE MY CHOOKS
TURNED INTO ROOSTERS AND KICK
THE CHOOK HOUSE DOWN FLY IN
THE OINTMENT RUN AROUND LIKE
A BLUE ARSED FLY WITHIN A BULL'S
ROAR **STARVE THE LIZARDS**
LIKE A BULL AT A GATE COCK AND
BULL SOMETHING THE CAT DRAGGED
IN DONE LIKE A DOG'S DINNER DEAD
AS A DODO STONE THE CROWS

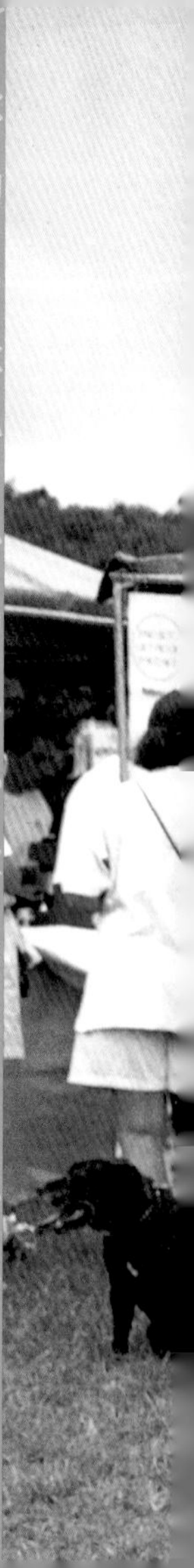

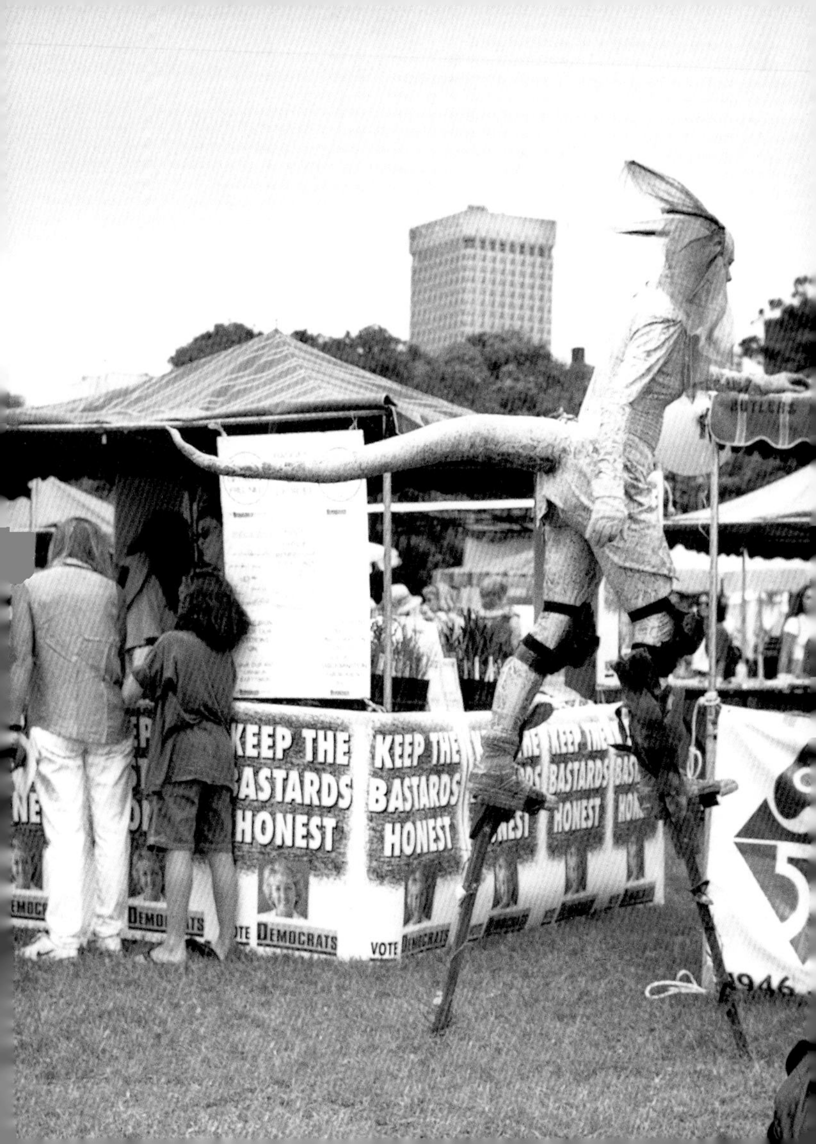
KEEP THE
BASTARDS
HONEST
DEMOCRATS
KEEP THE
BASTARDS
HONEST
VOTE DEMOCRATS
BUTLERS

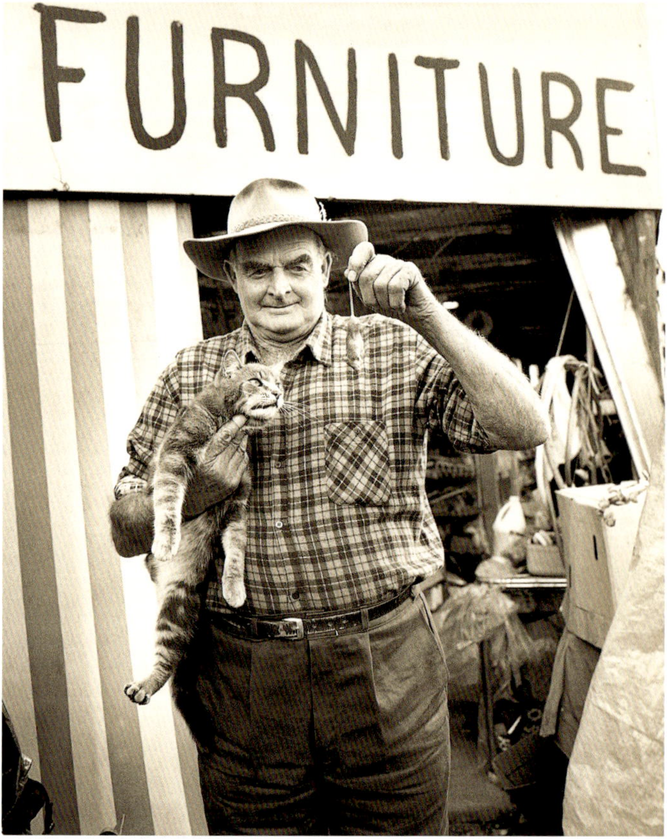

CAT AND MOUSE
Dimboola

BEN "SMILING"
Lindfield

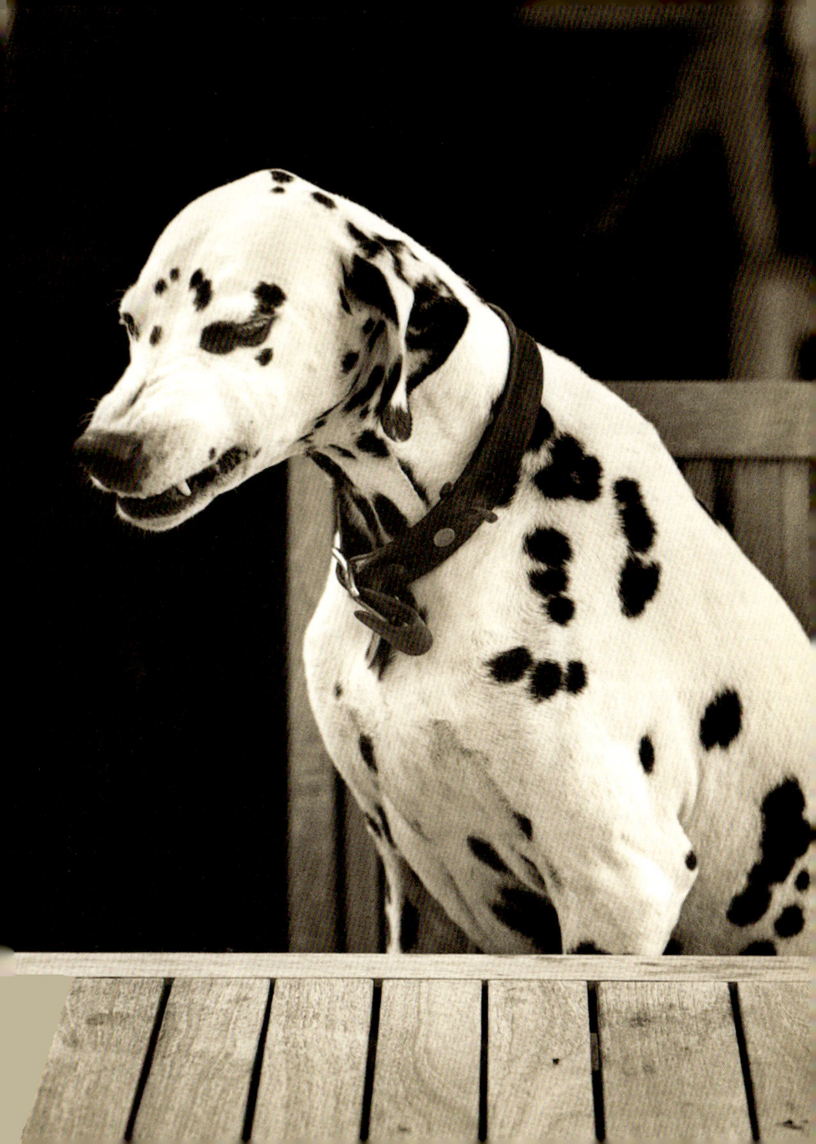

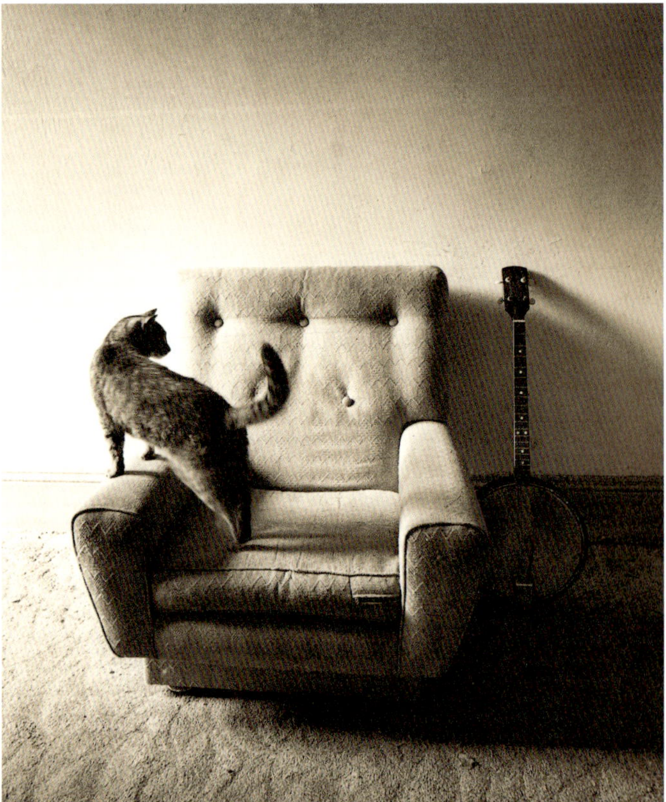

Glebe

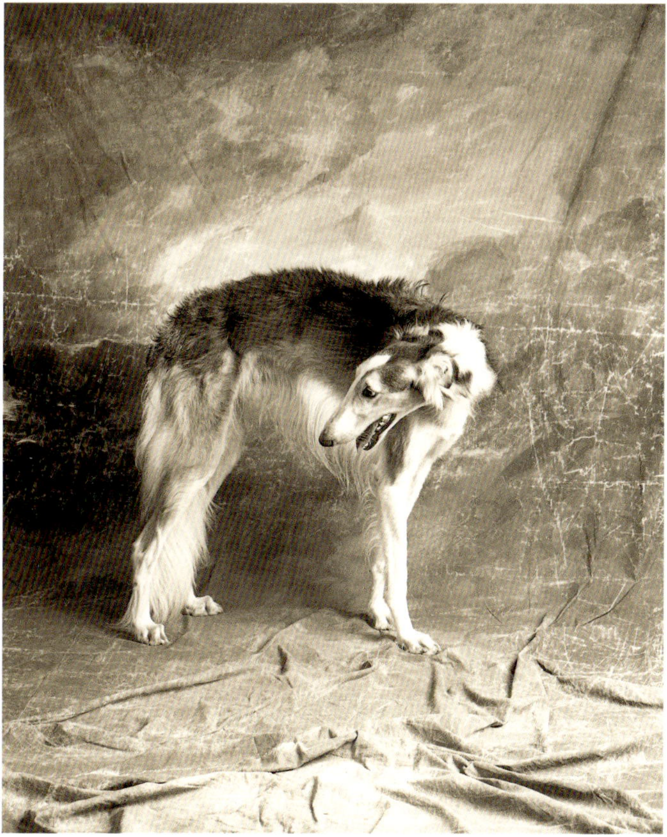

BORZOI

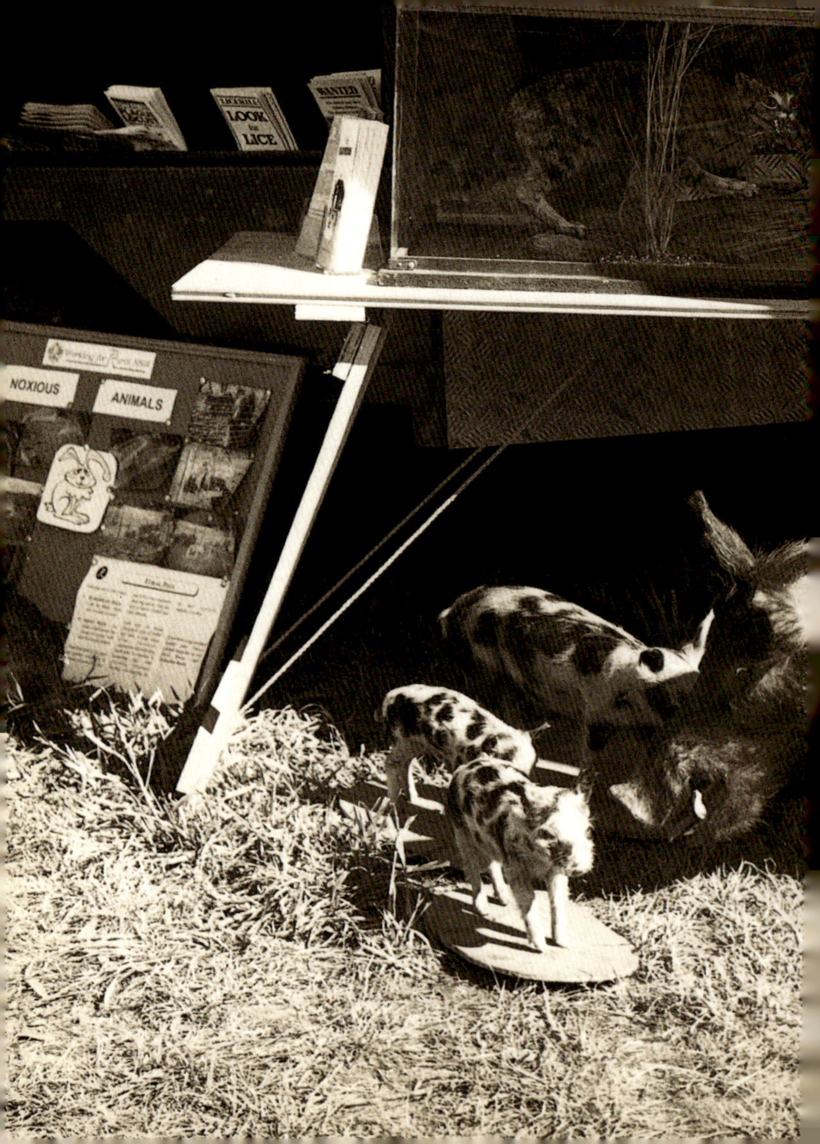
LOOK
LICE
WANTED
NOXIOUS
ANIMALS

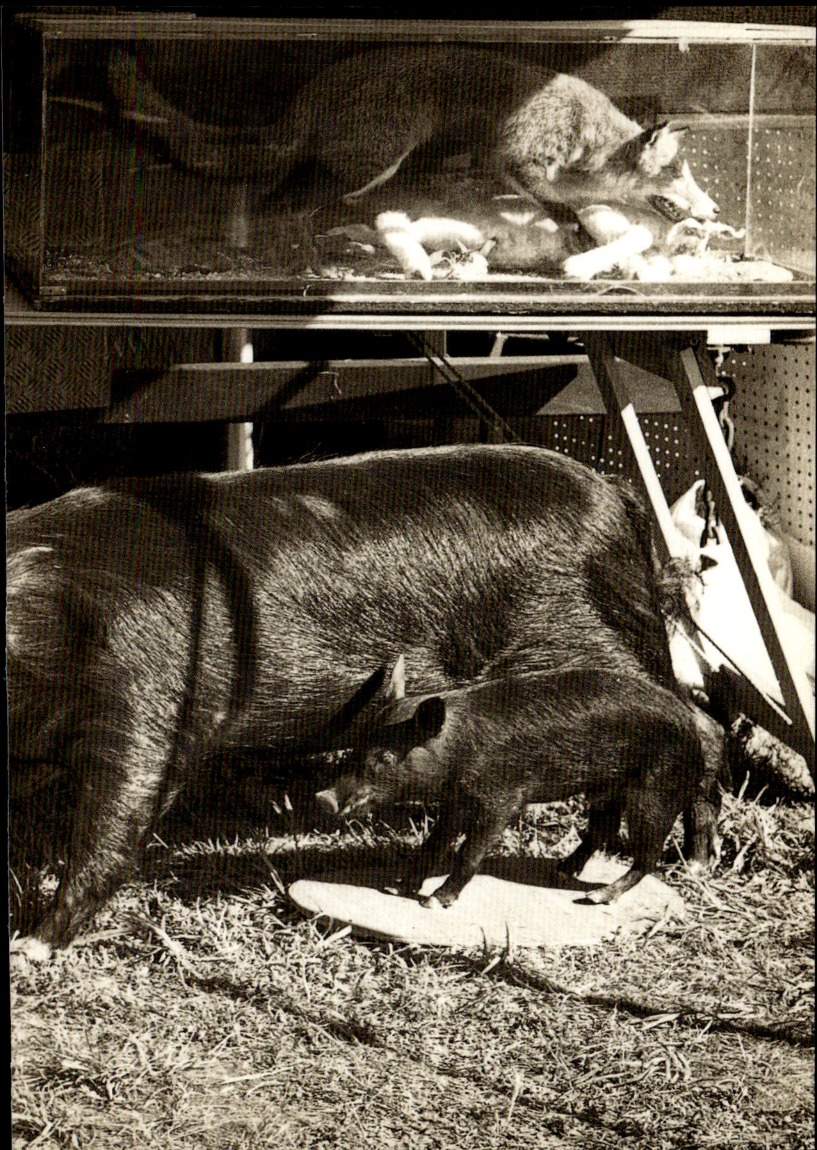

Previous page:
Murrumbateman Show, NSW

So hot the fleas and
flies have bloodshot
eyes from squinting.

CICADAS

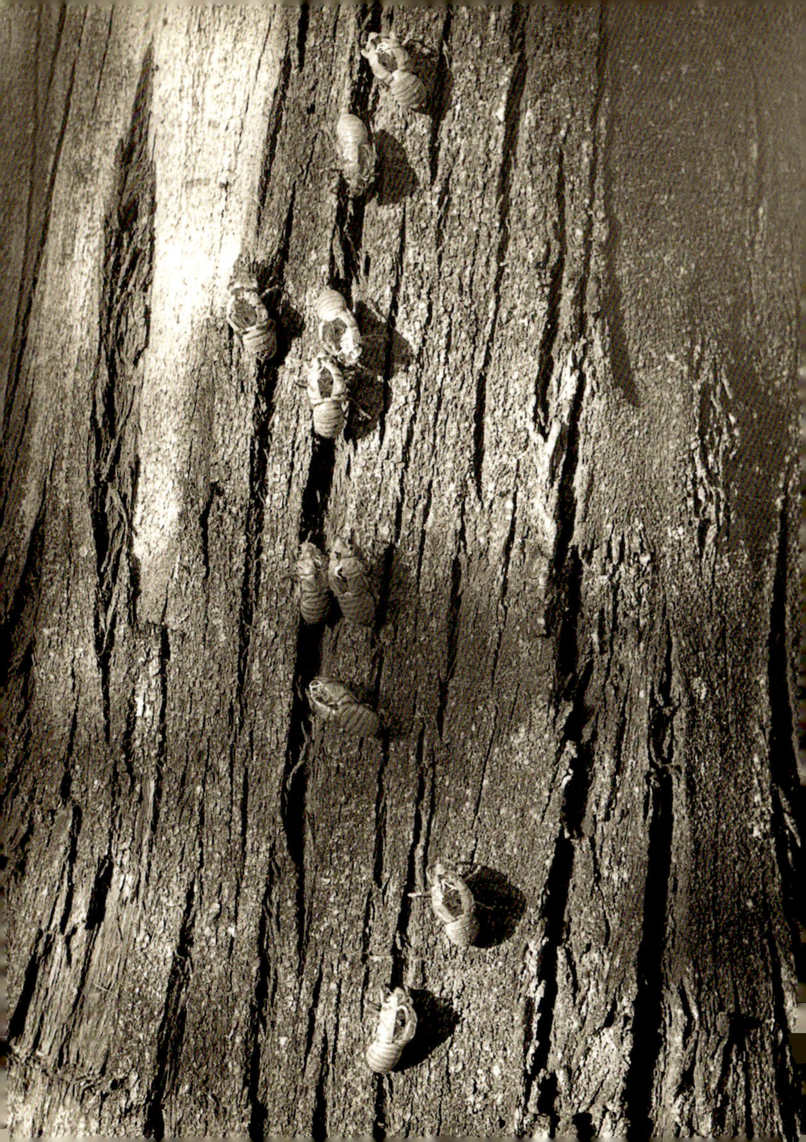

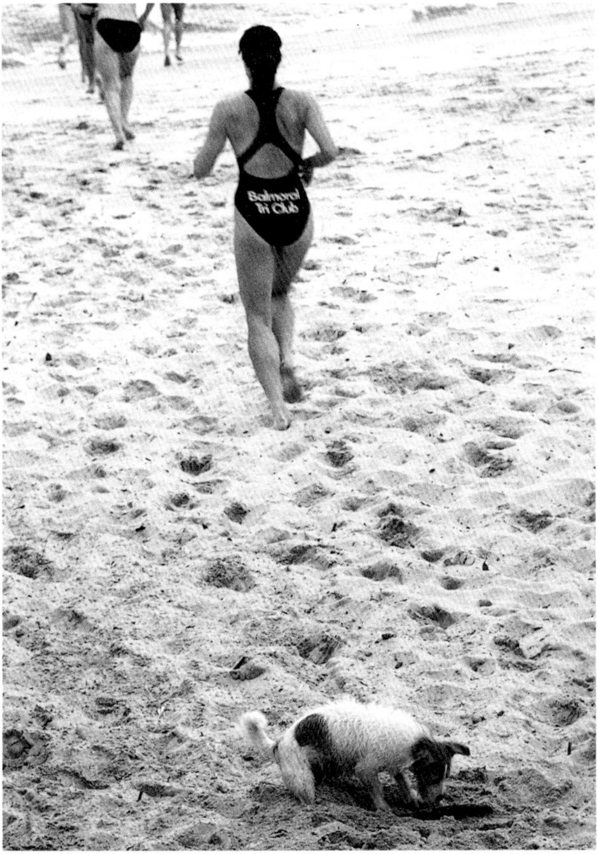

GIVE A DOG A BONE

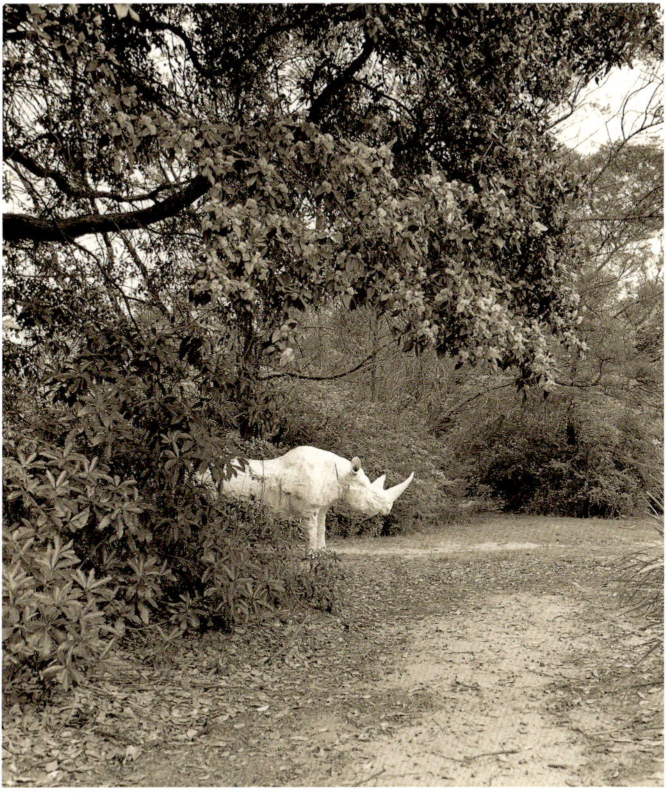

FEELING HORNY
Arcadia

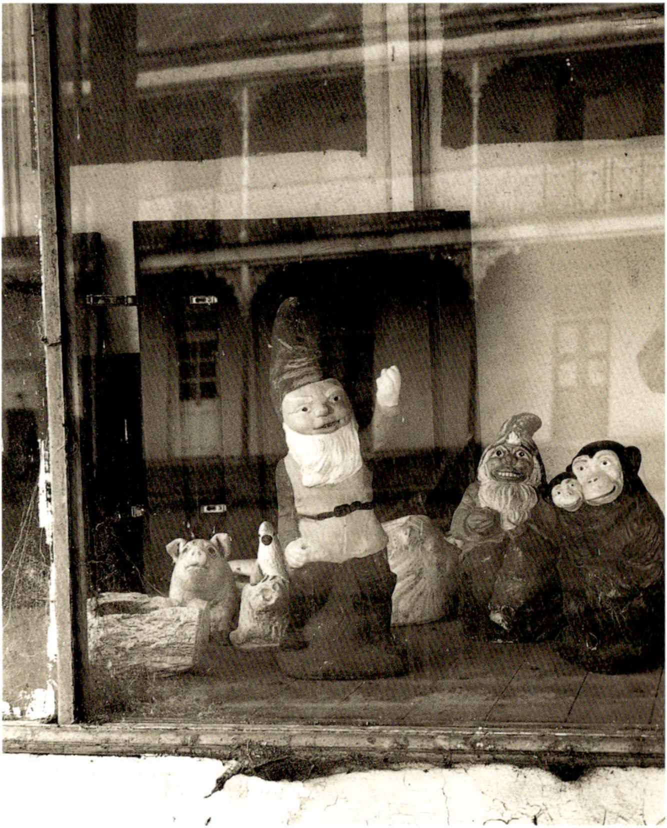

I'LL BE A MONKEYS UNCLE
Scone

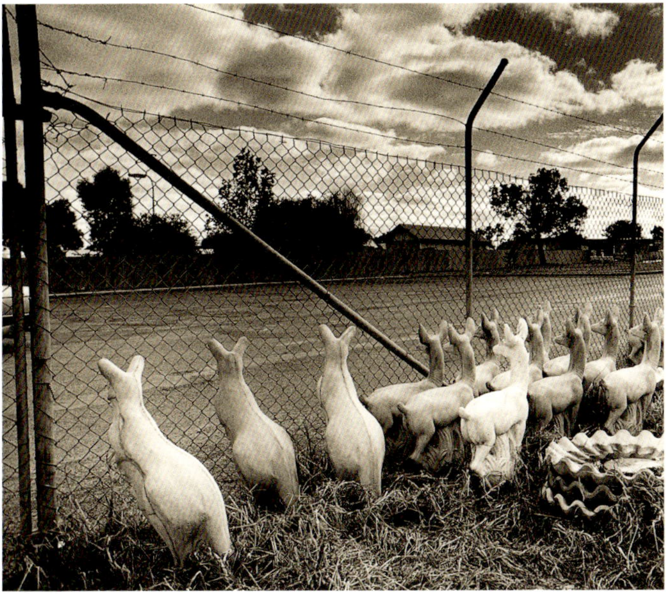

SHUFTI – HAVE A LOOK
Condobolin

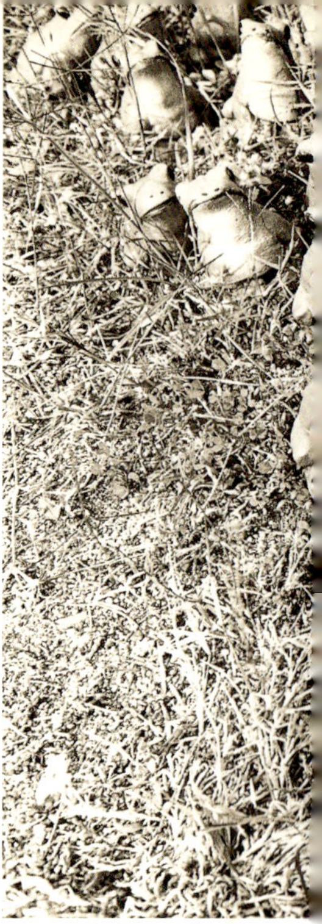

GREEN TREE FROGS

So dry that there's a
family of frogs under
the house and none of
'em can swim

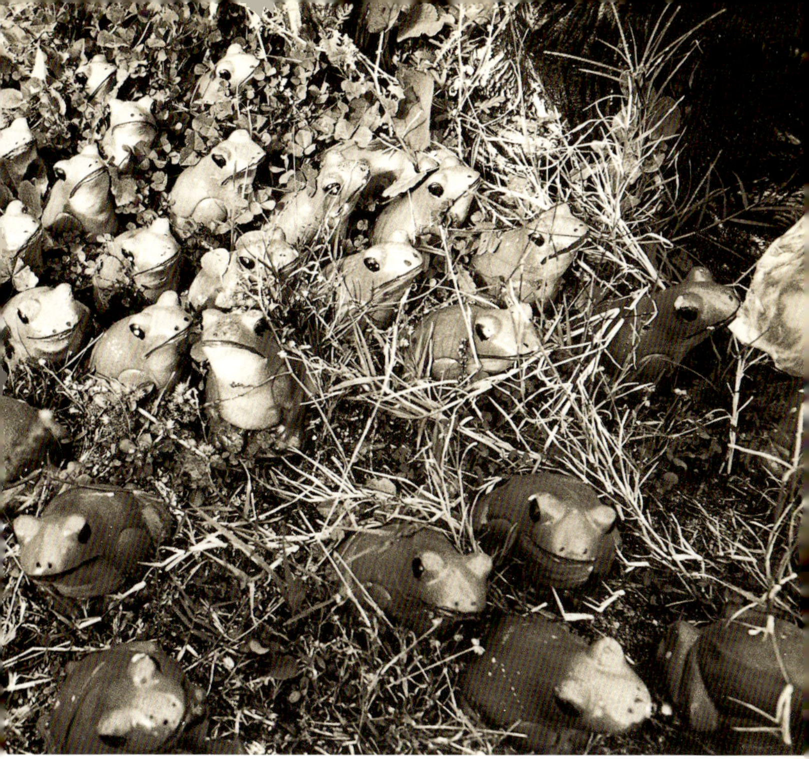

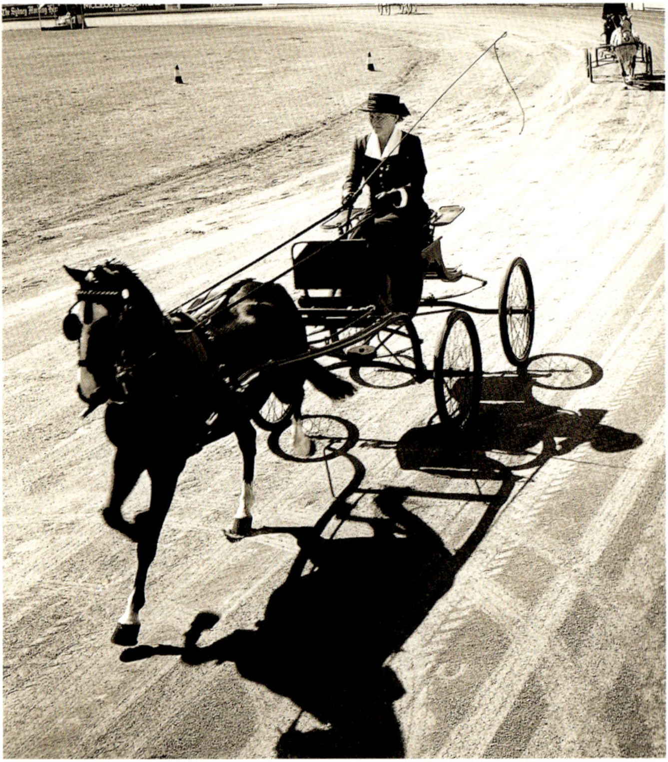

Homebush, NSW

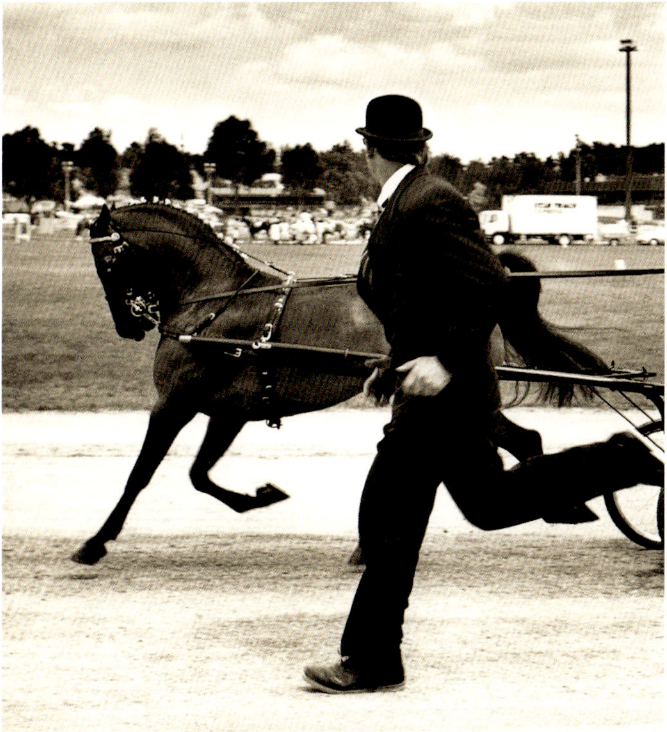

ON THE TROT
Canberra

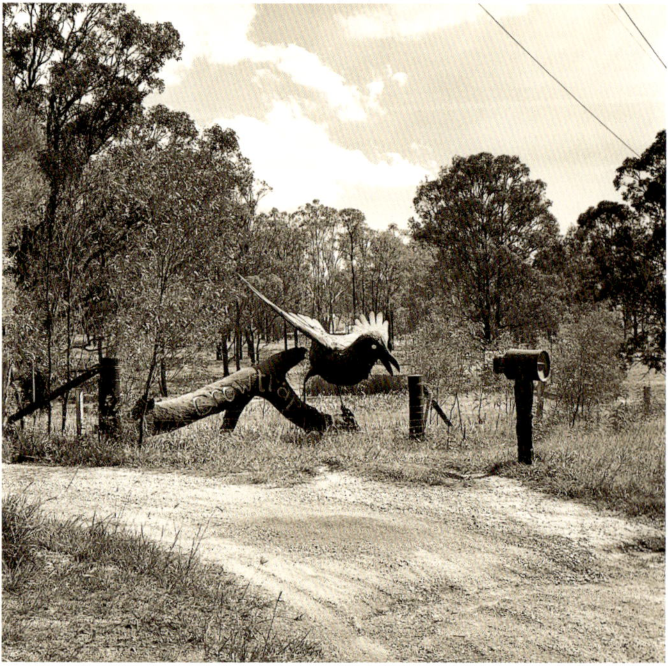

STANDS OUT LIKE A BLACK CROW IN
A BUCKET OF MILK
Hunter Valley

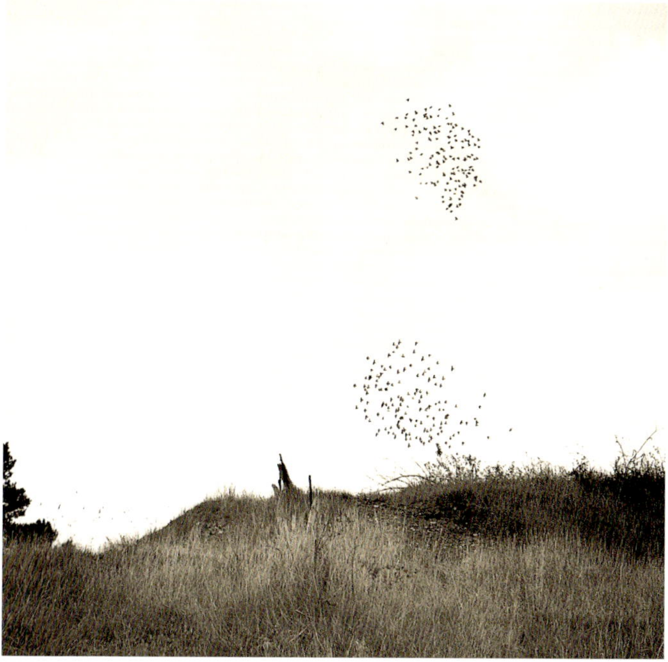

Orange Country

Flying on a wing
or a prayer

Rose Bay

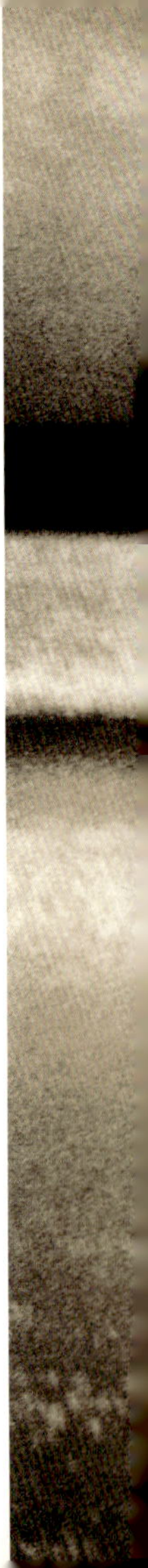

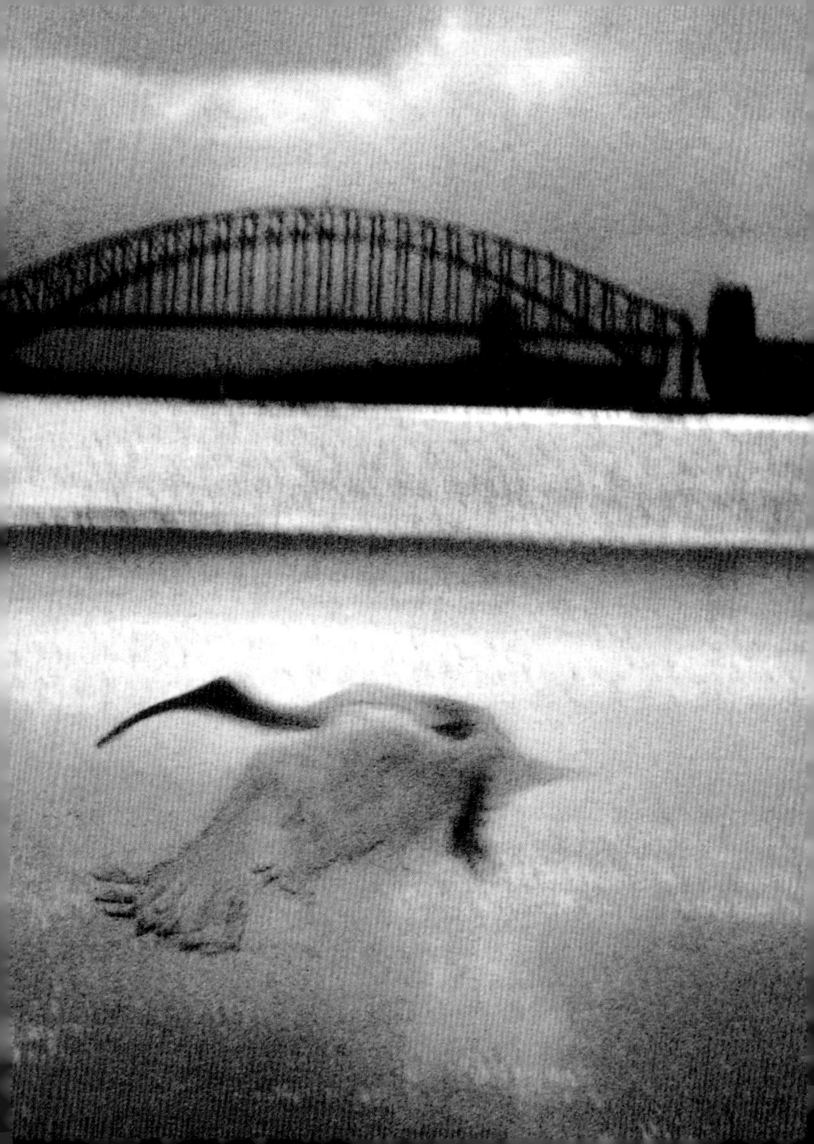

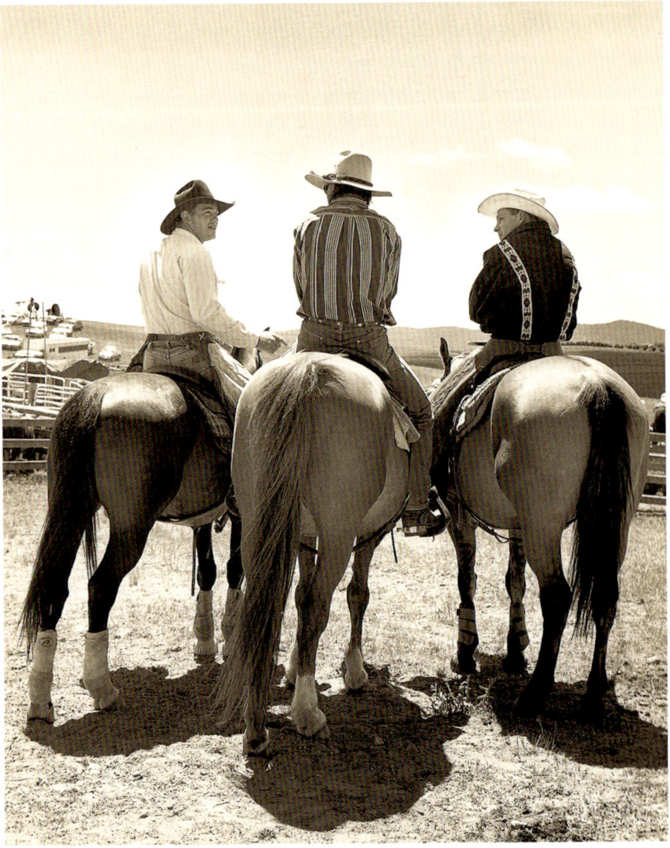

Bungendore Rodeo

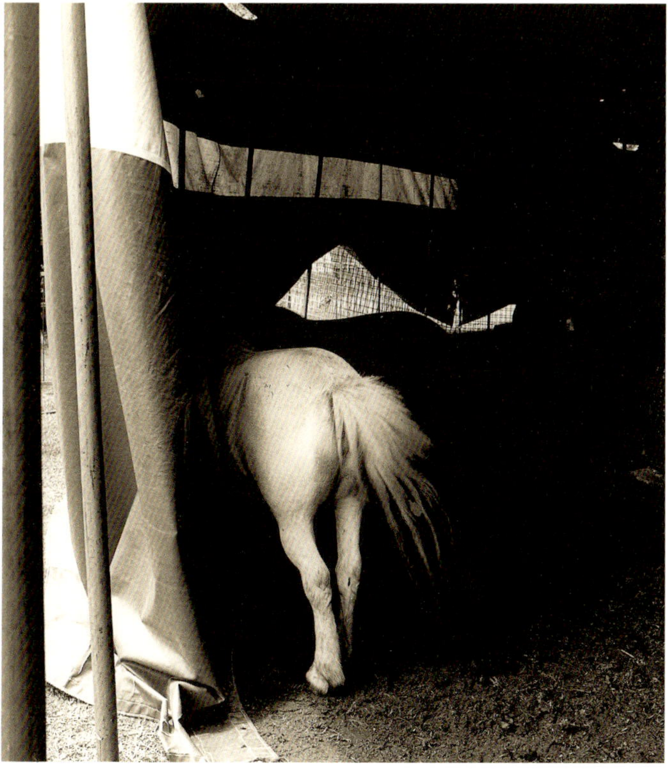

AS ATTRACTIVE AS A HORSE'S ...

Overleaf:
Alpacas, Marulan

DRUNK AS A SKUNK **AWAY WITH THE BIRDS** PISSED AS A PARROT **HAVE A HAIR OF THE DOG** MOUTH WILL FEEL LIKE THE BOTTOM OF A COCKY'S CAGE **MY CHOOKS TURNED INTO ROOSTERS AND KICK THE CHOOK HOUSE DOWN** FLY IN THE OINTMENT **RUN AROUND LIKE A BLUE ARSED FLY** WITH IN A BULL'S ROAR **STARVE THE LIZARDS** LIKE A BULL AT A GATE **COCK AND BULL** SOMETHING THE CAT DRAGGED IN **DONE LIKE A DOG'S DINNER** DEAD AS A DODO **STONE THE CROWS** KNEE HIGH TO A GRASSHOPPER **JUST BEES KNEES** HE WOULDN'T SHOUT IN A SHARK ATTACK

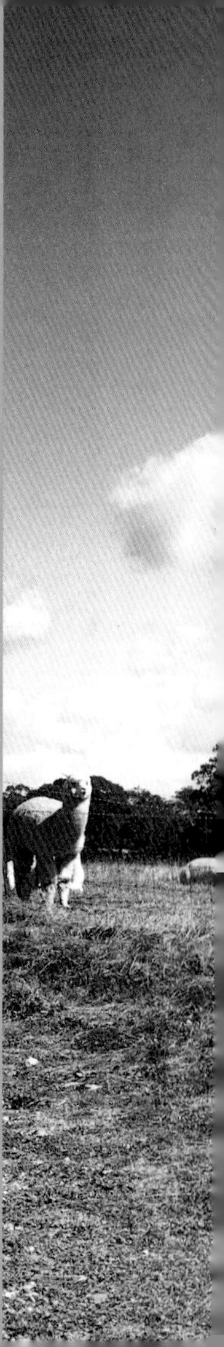

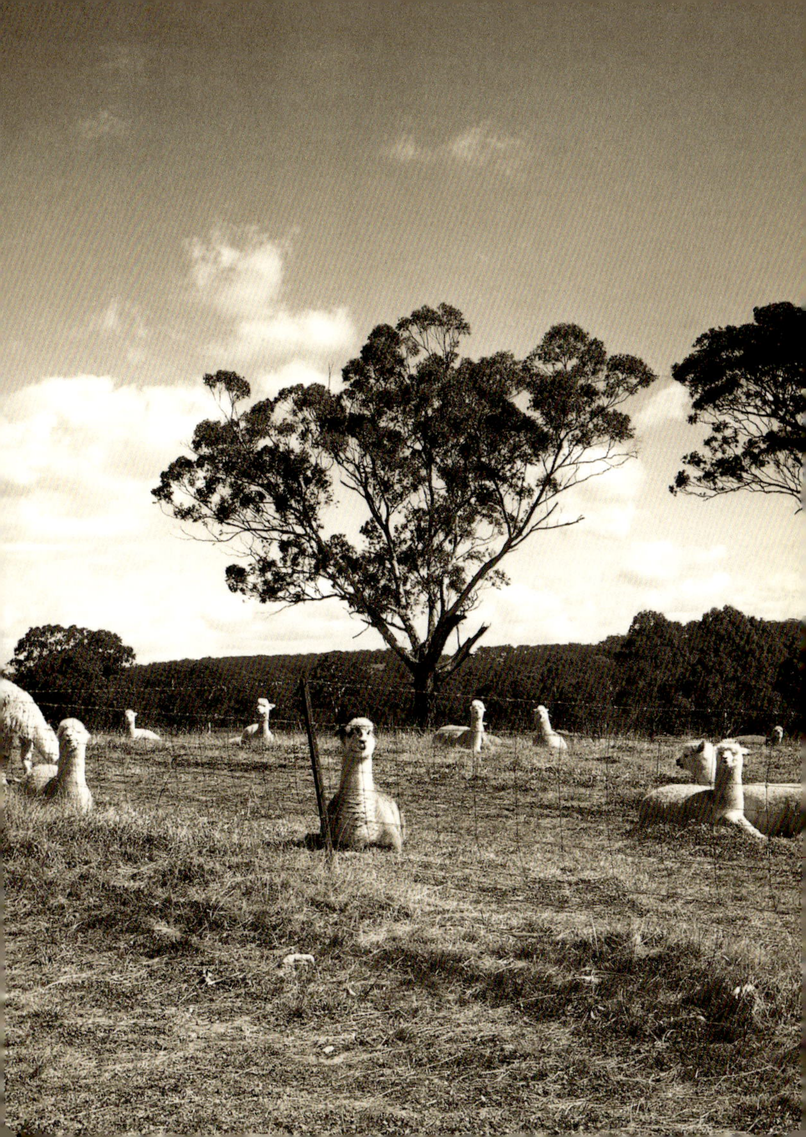

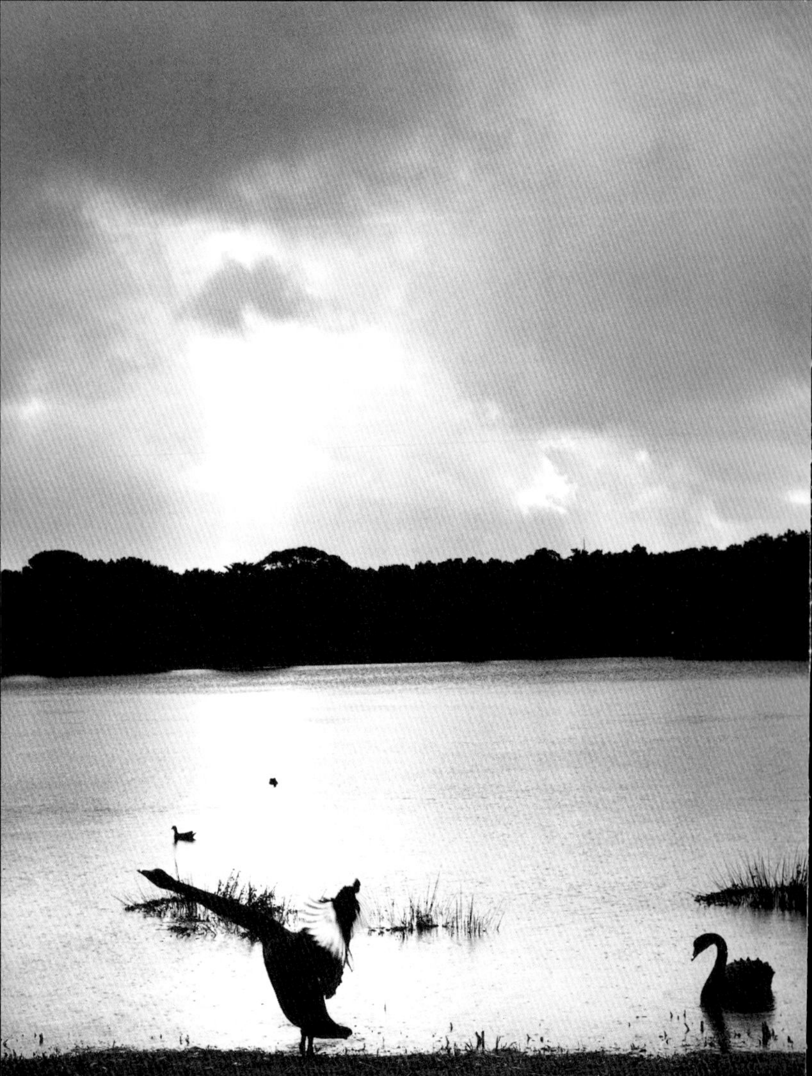

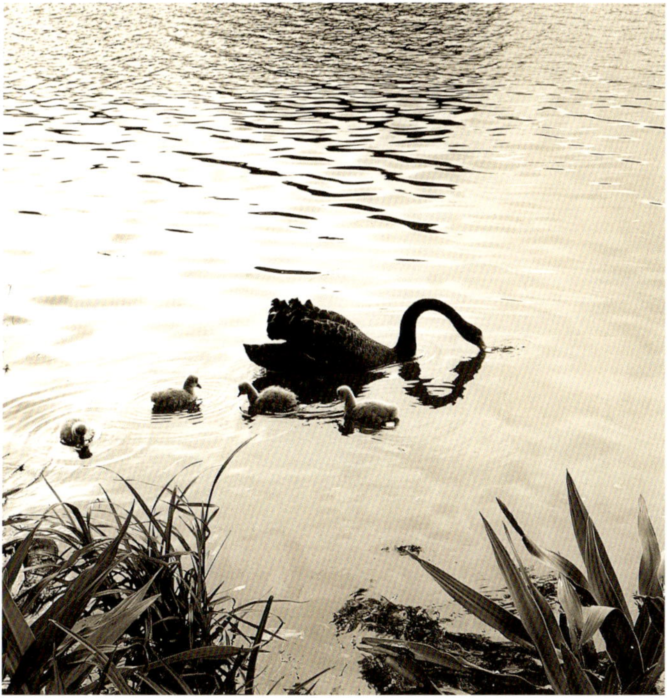

WITHIN COOEE
Centennial Park

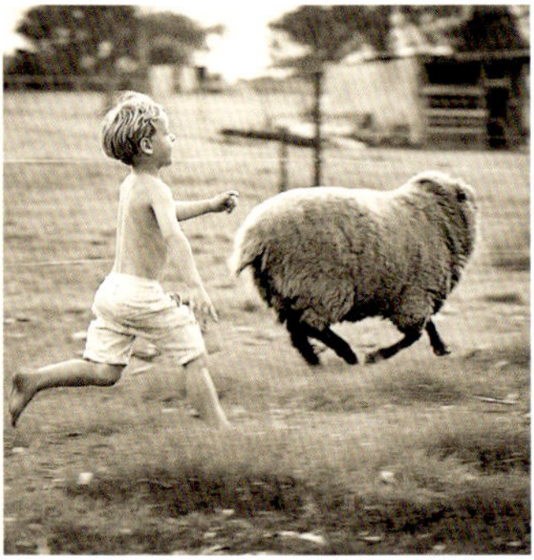

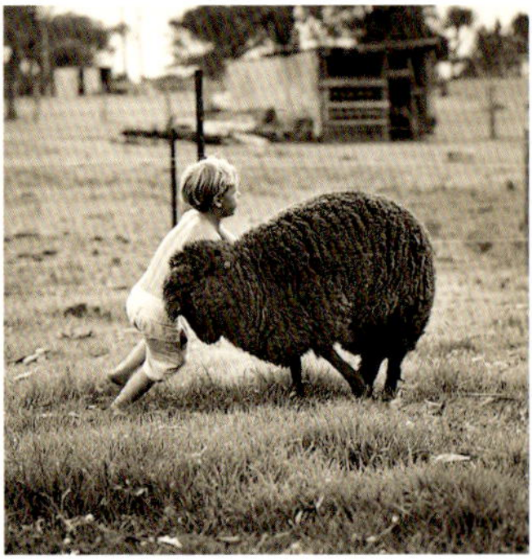

CATCH ME IF YOU CAN

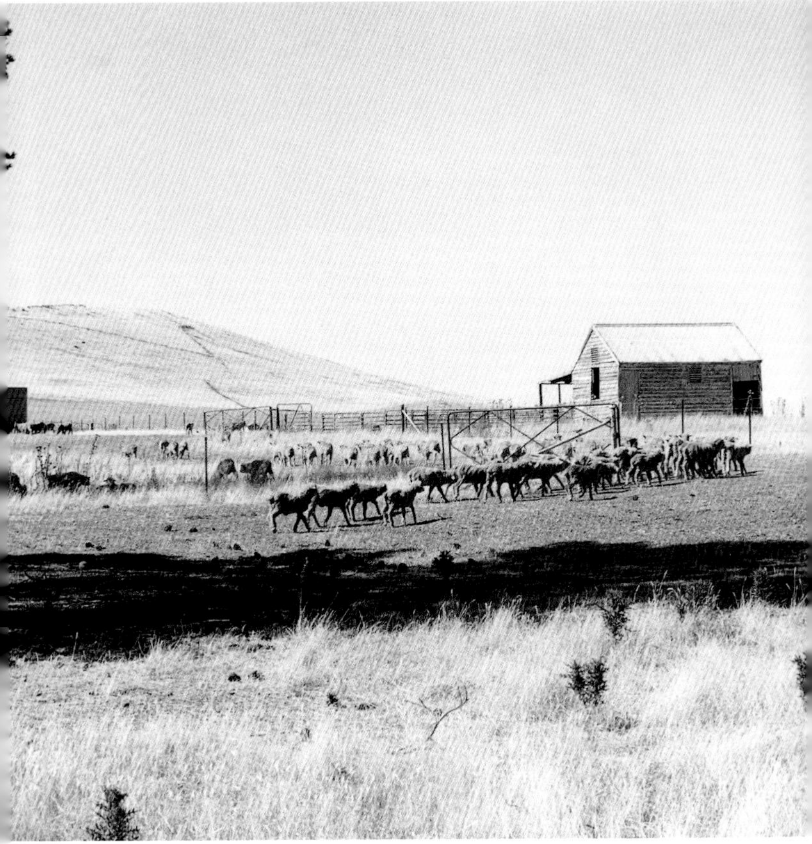

MUTTON DRESSED UP AS LAMB

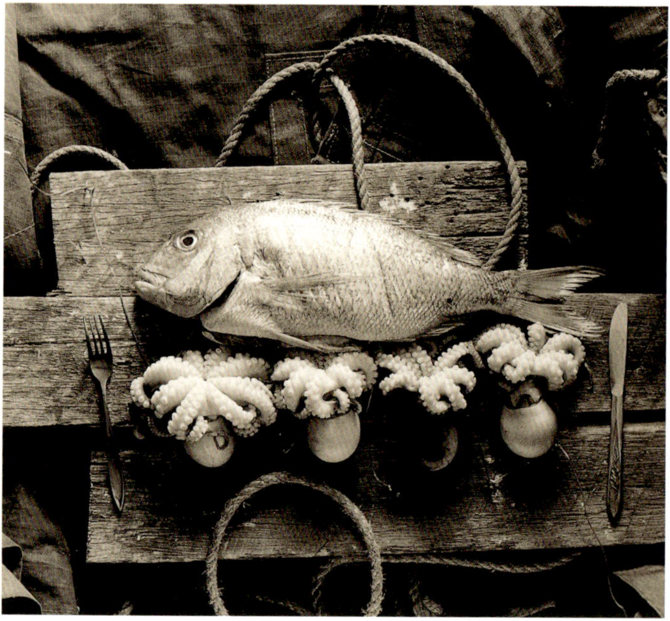

PLAY ME A DIFFERENT TUNA

Dee Why

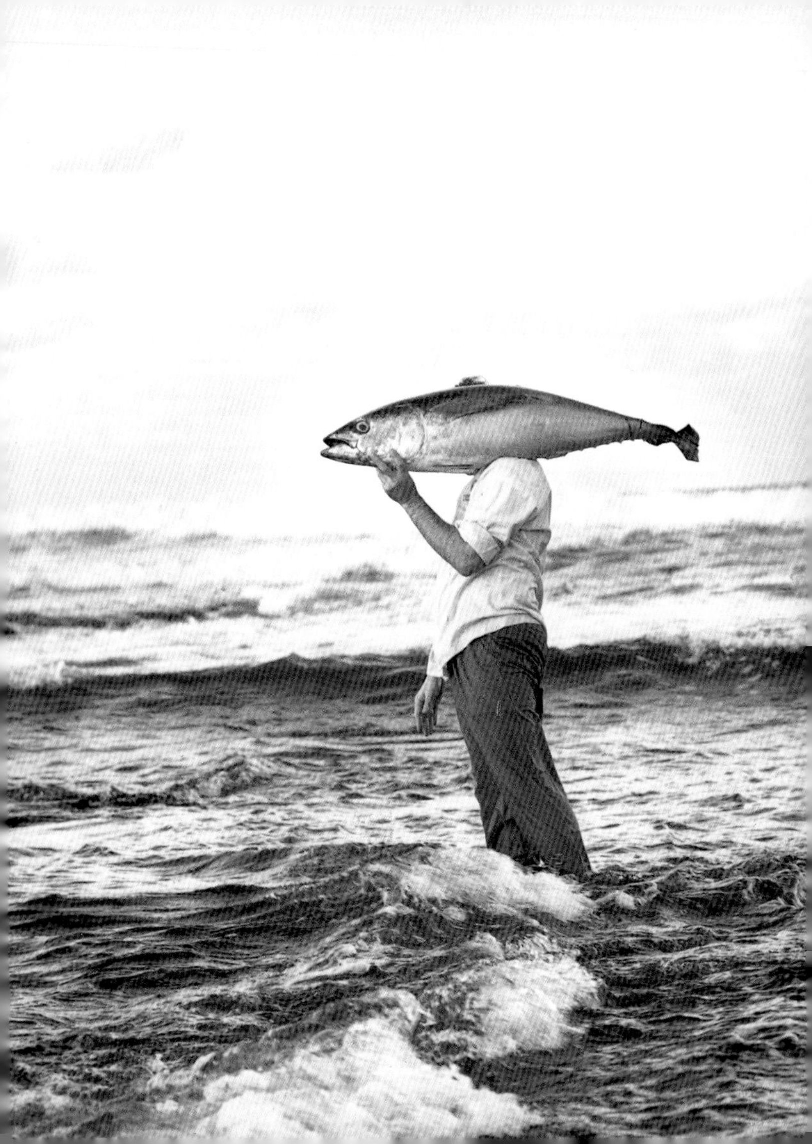

So hungry, I could
eat the crotch out of
a low flying duck.

SITTING DUCKS
Arcadia

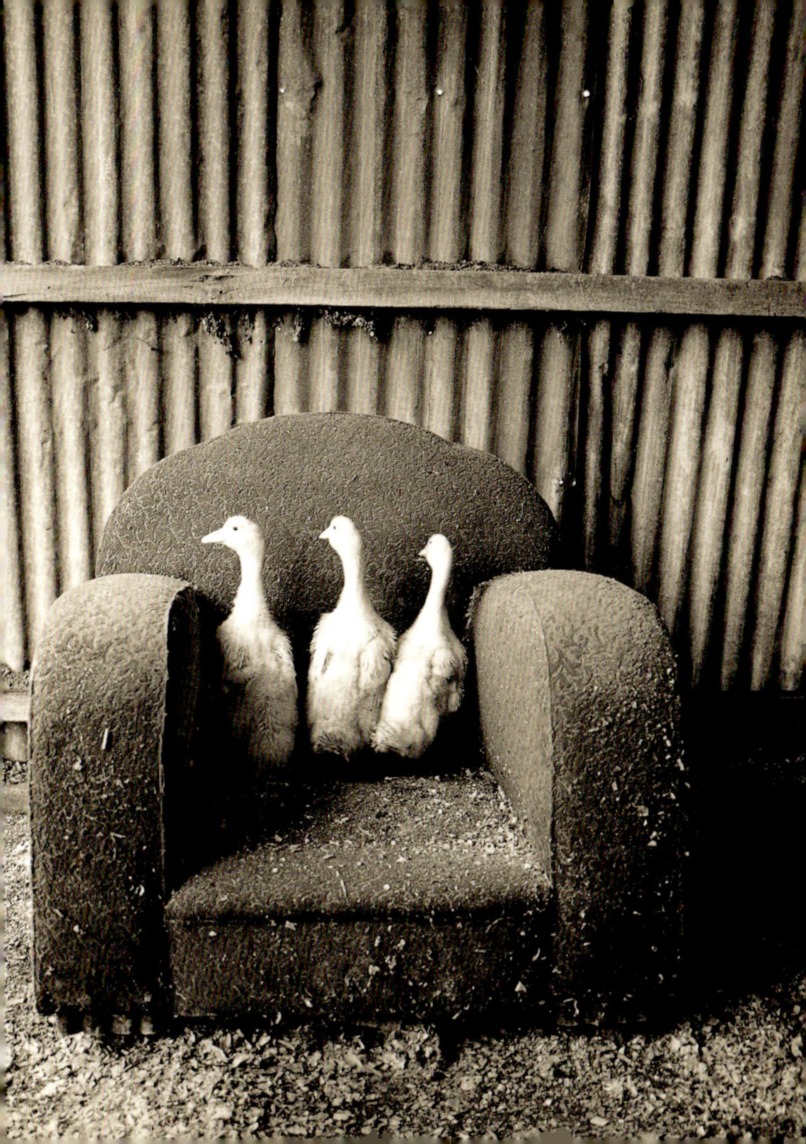

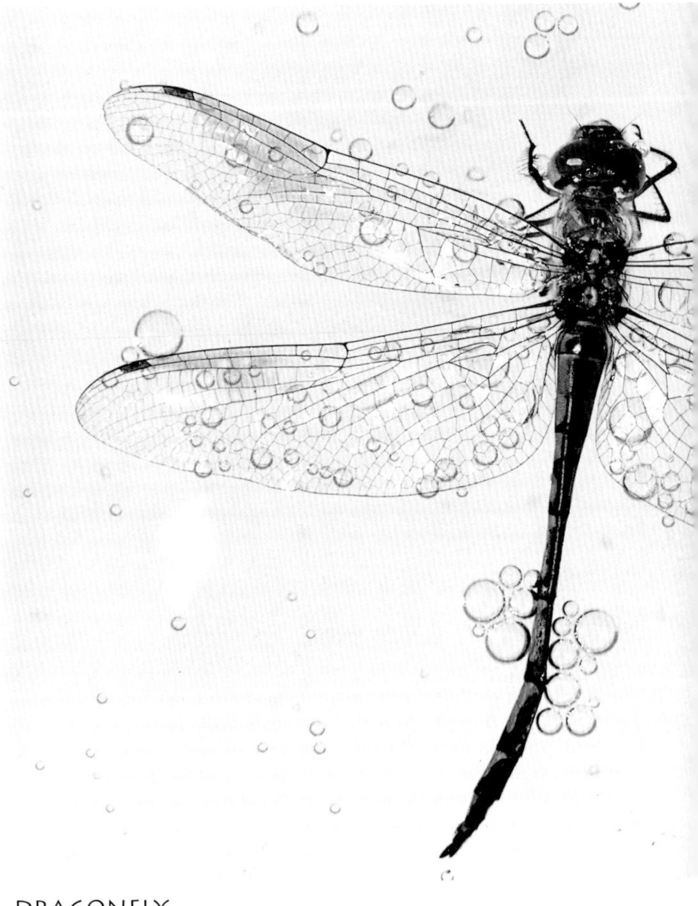

DRAGONFLY

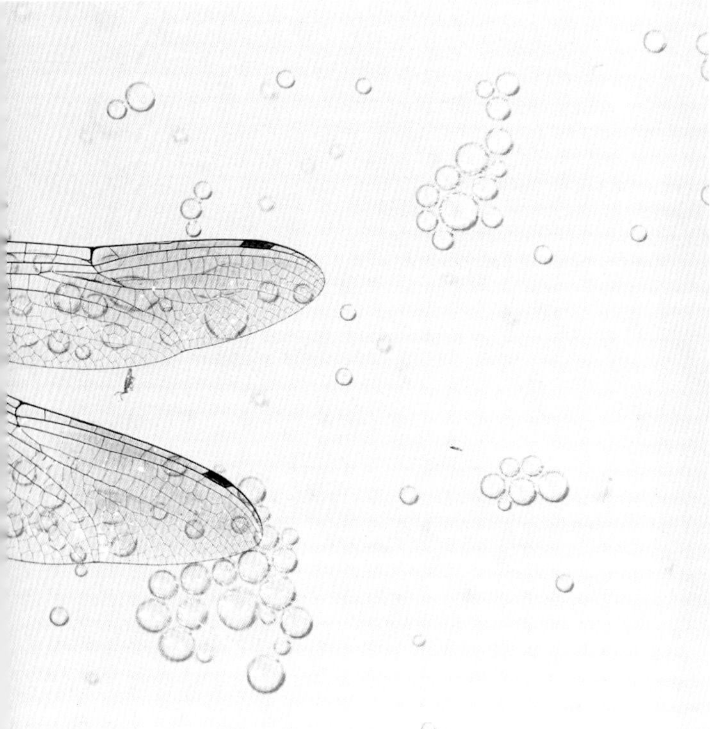

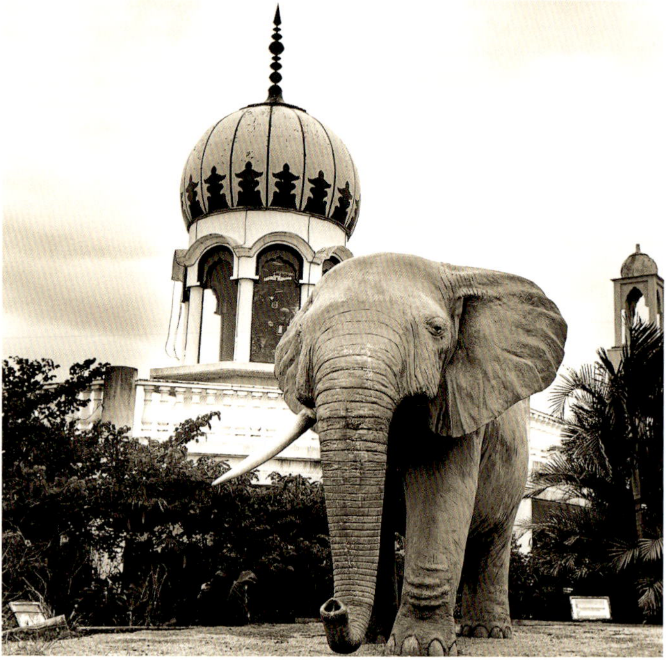

On the way to Byron Bay

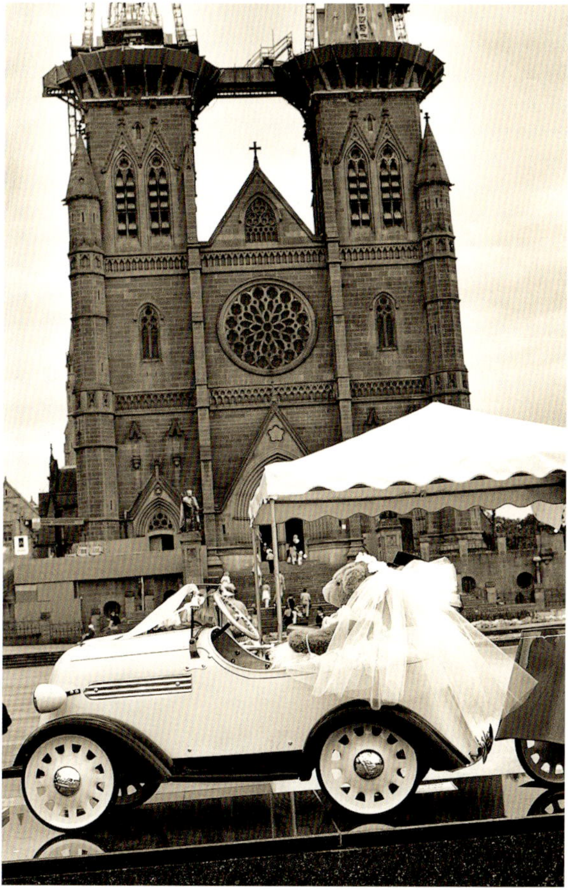

TIE THE KNOT
St Marys Cathedral

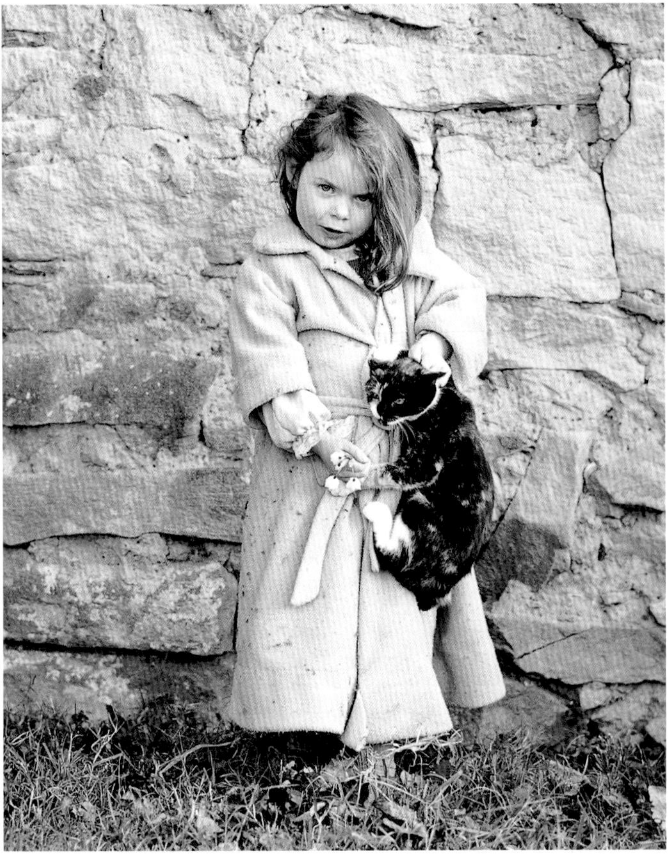

MOGGY

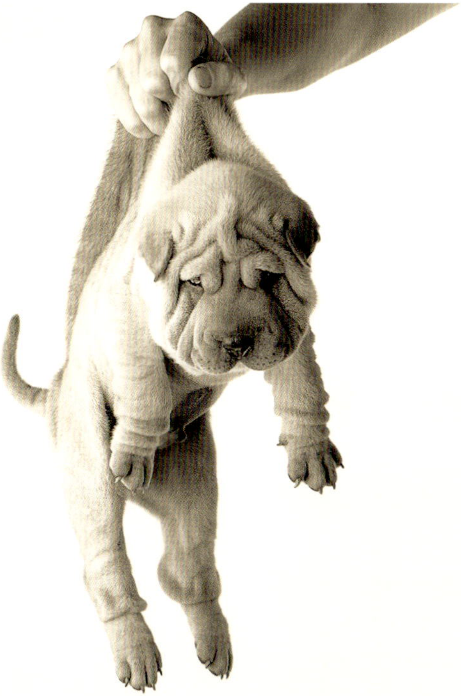

PARACHUTE POOCH

Overleaf:
GREYHOUND RACE, Moss Vale

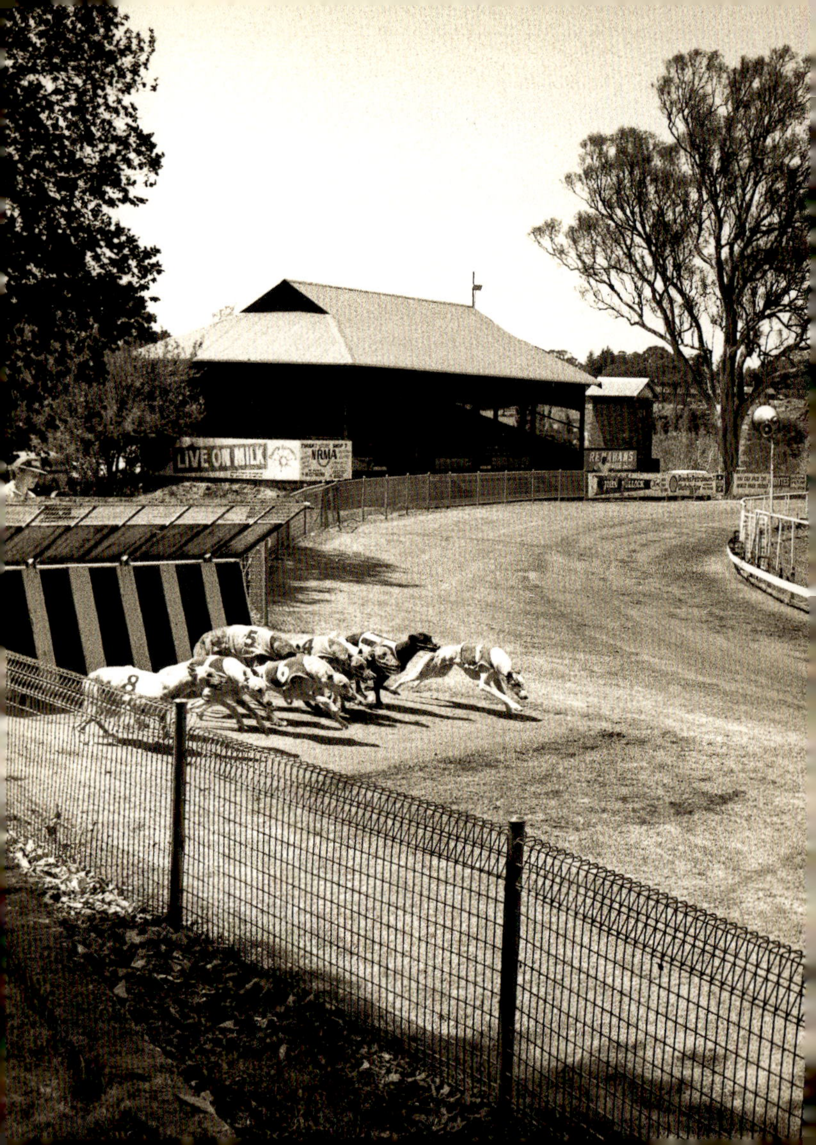
LIVE ON MILK
NRMA

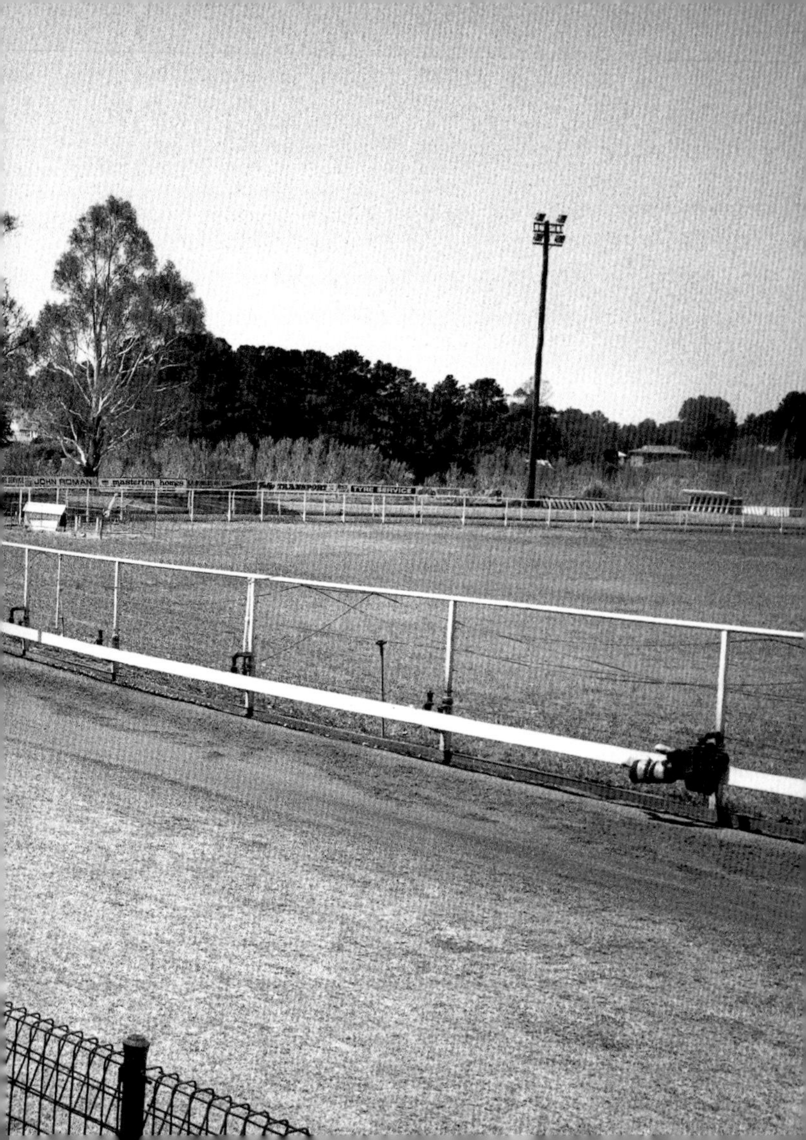

JOHN ROMAN
masterton homes
TRANSPORT
TYRE SERVICE

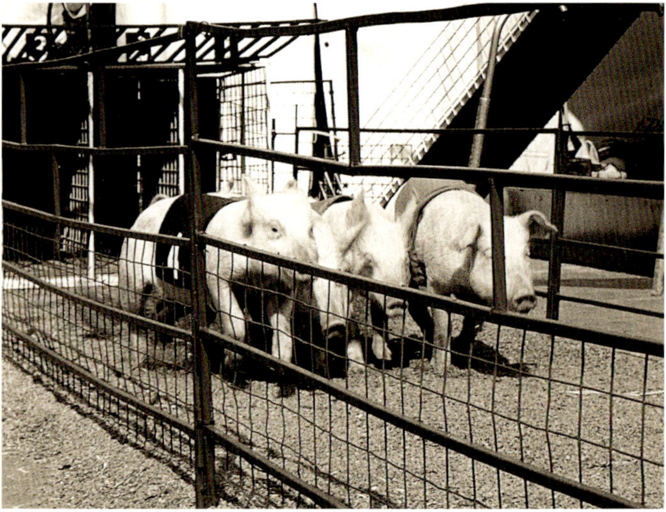

Easter Show, Sydney

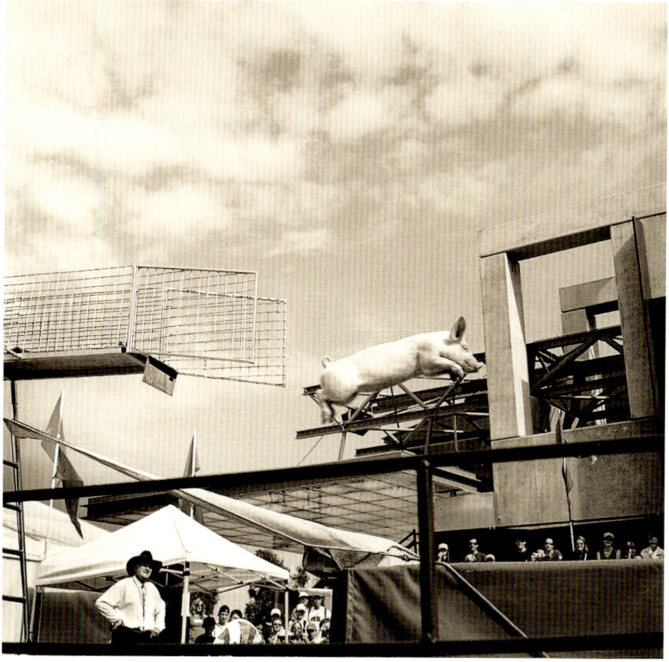

FLYING PIG:
BRITISH 9.45" TRENCH MORTAR BOMB

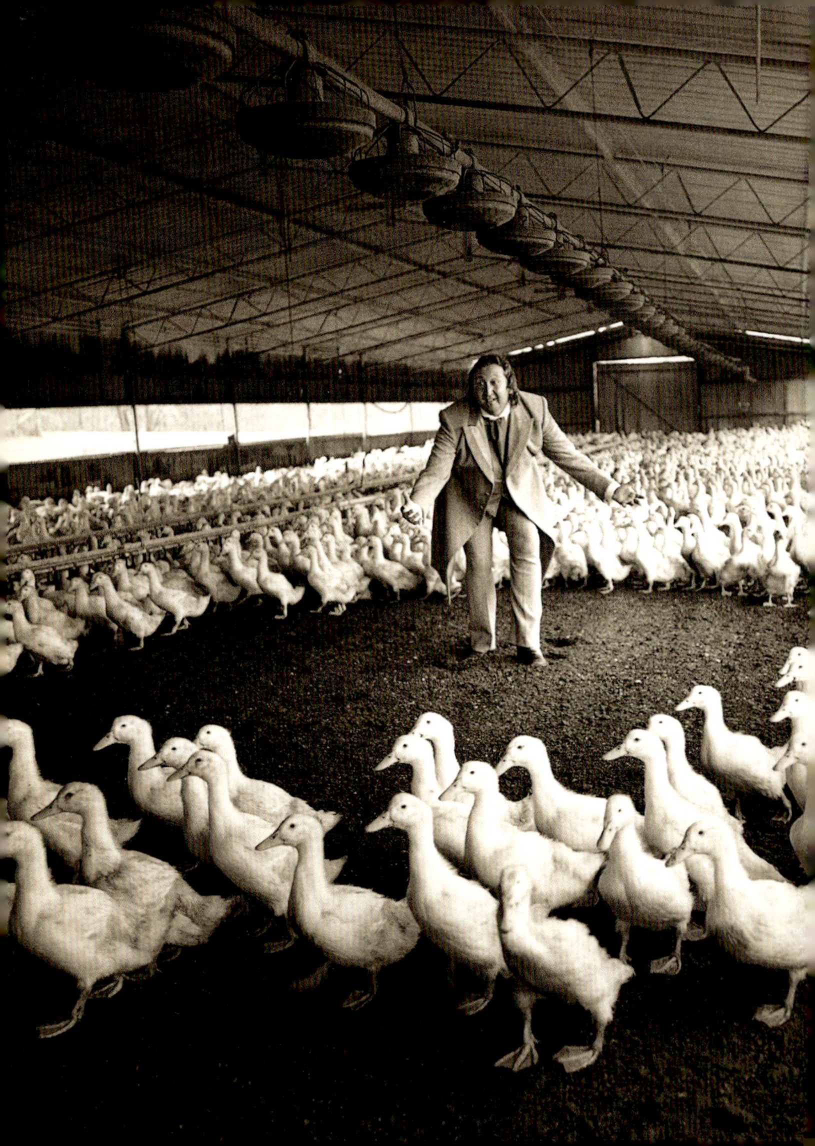

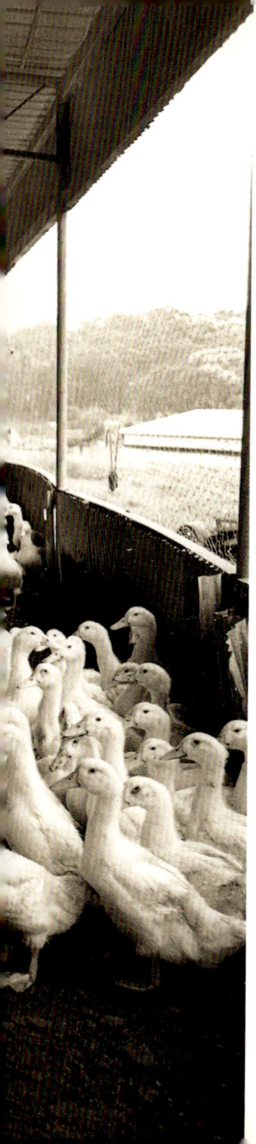

YOU'LL LOVE IT HERE, TRUST ME

Arcadia

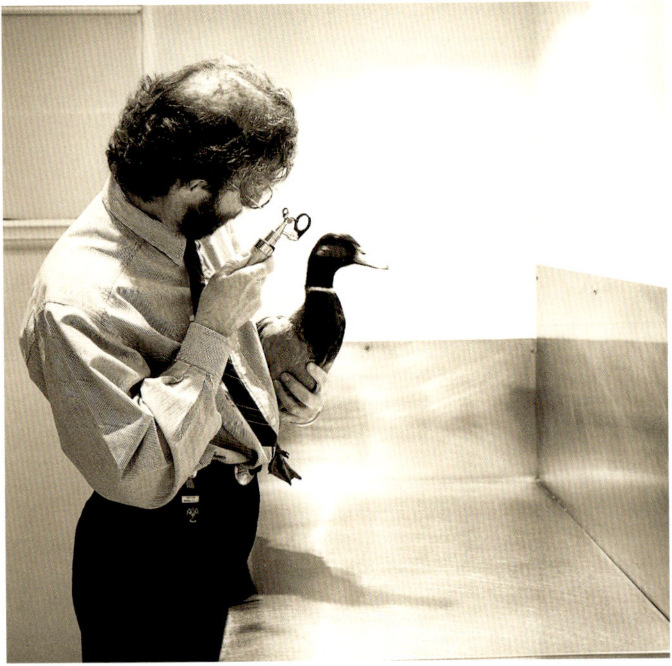

YEP, IT'S A DUCK ALRIGHT
Carlingford

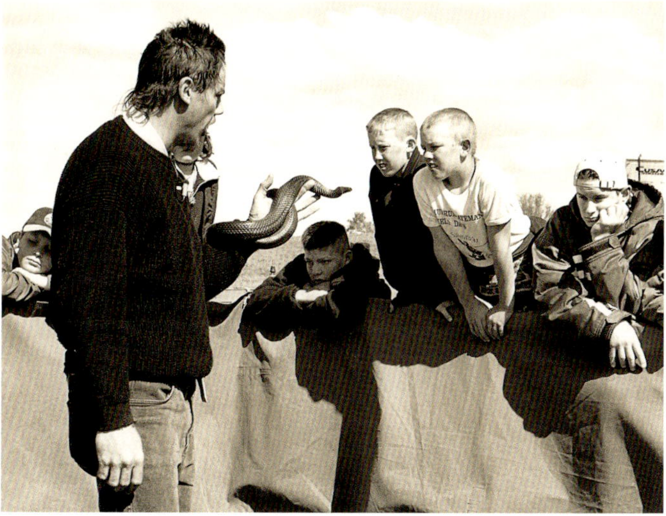

MAD AS A CUT SNAKE
Murrumbateman

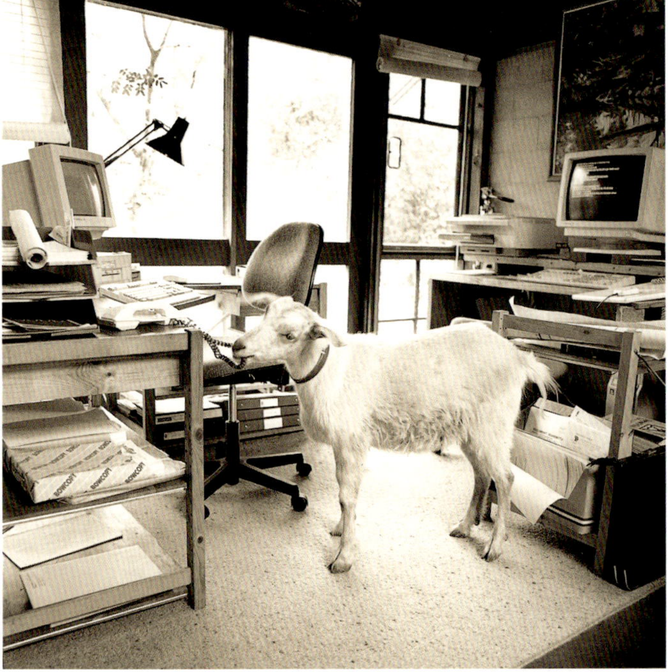

ACTING THE GOAT

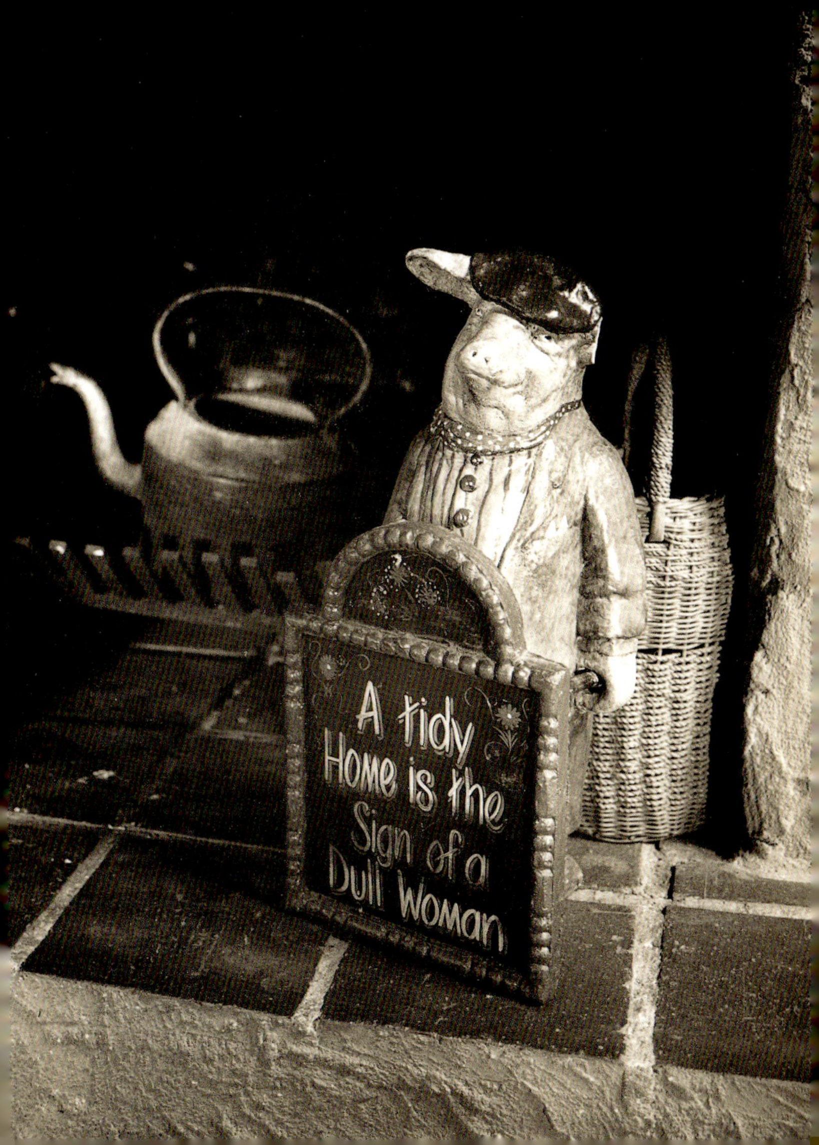
A tidy
Home is the
Sign of a
Dull Woman

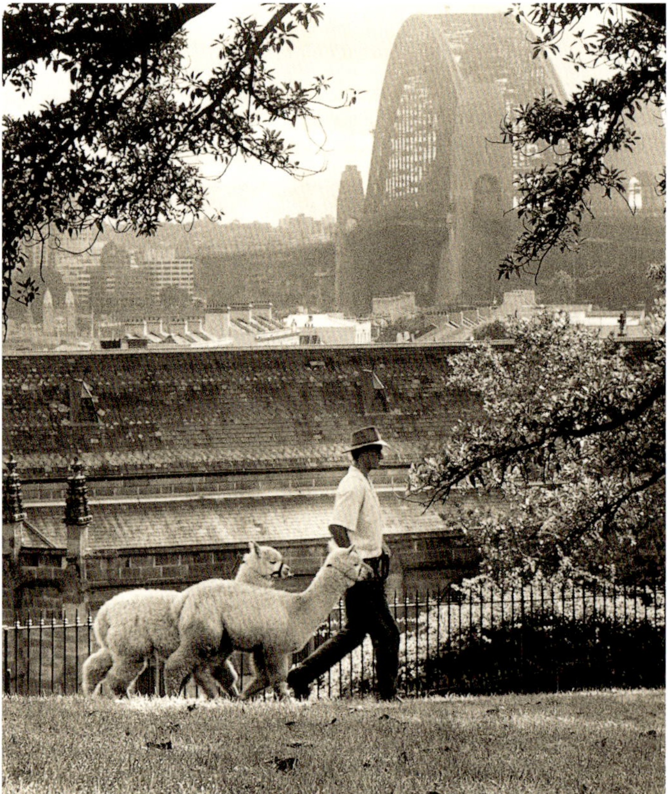

ALPACAS ON HOLIDAYS

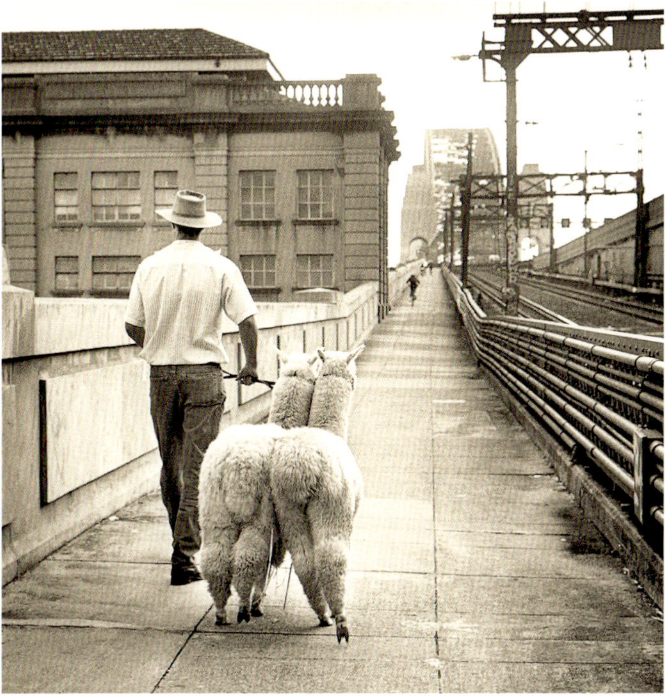

A BRIDGE TOO FAR

STREET WALKER
Crows Nest

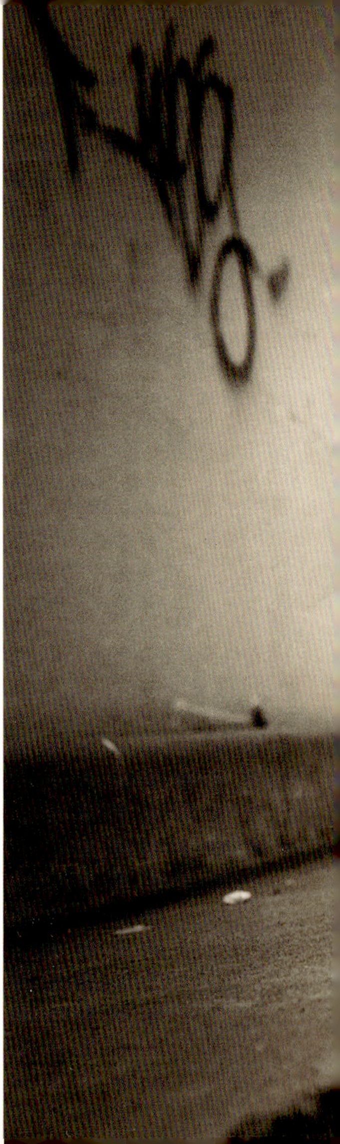

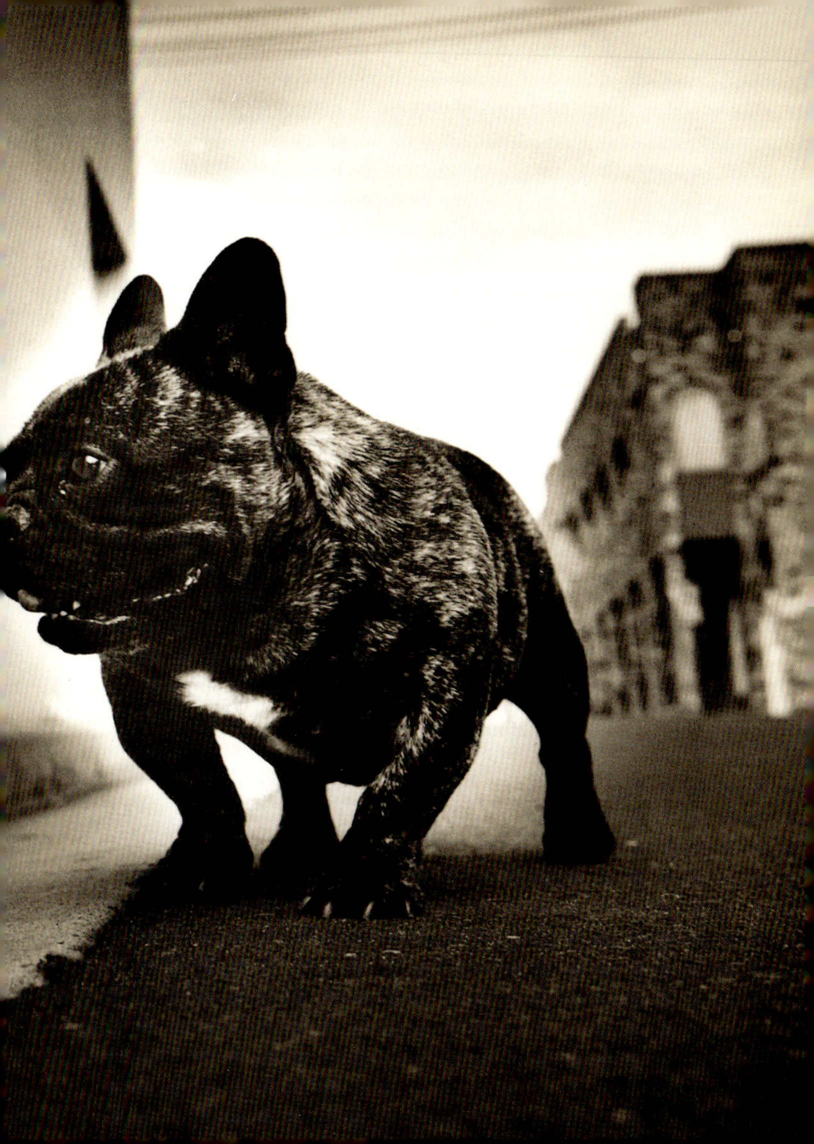

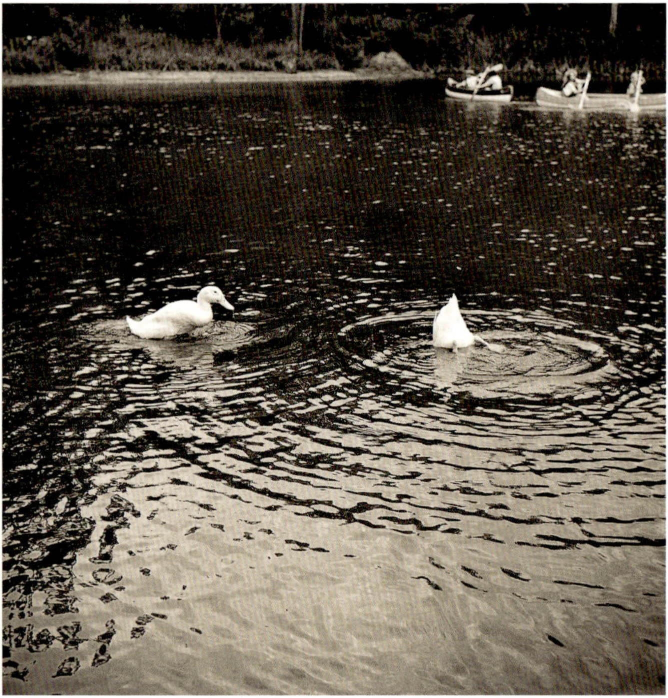

BOTTOMS UP
Galston

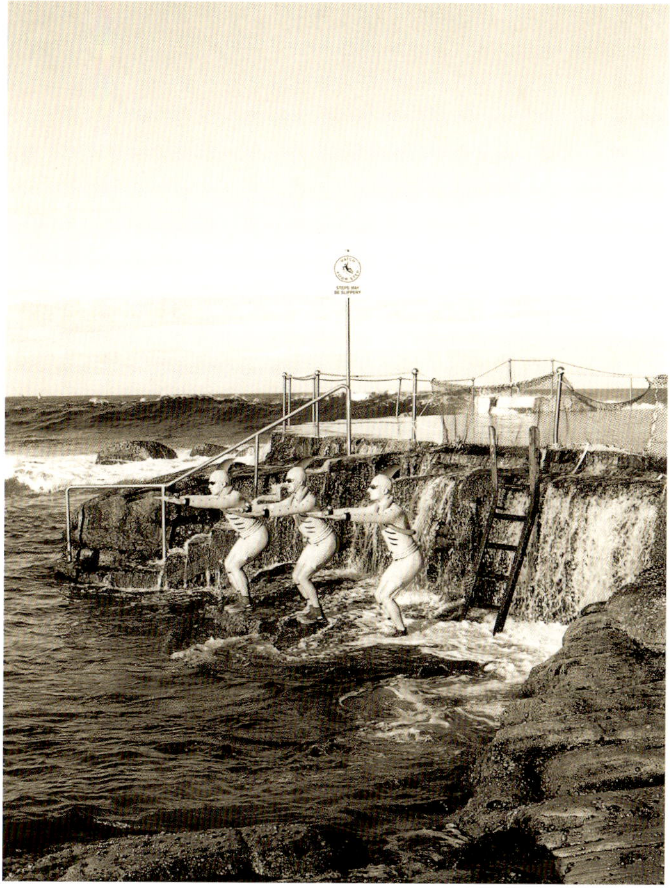

WON'T SHOUT IN A SHARK ATTACK
Bronte

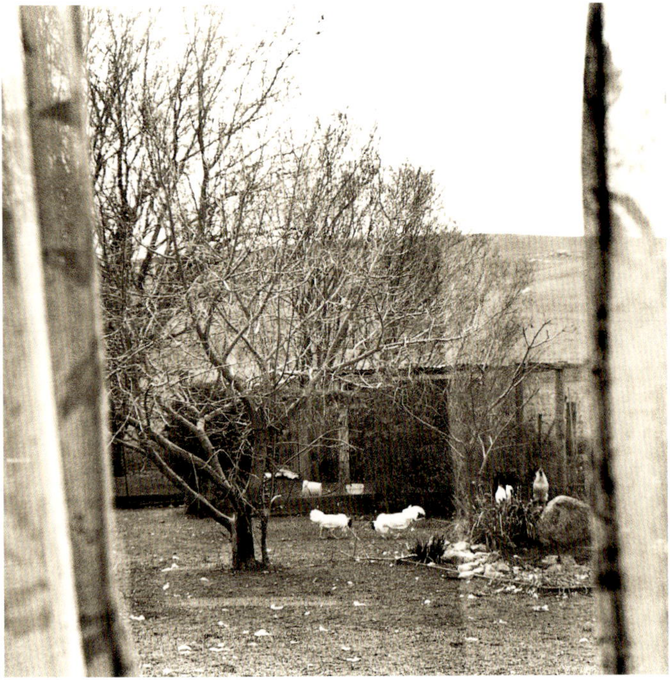

I HOPE YOUR CHOOKS TURN INTO
EMUS AND KICK YOUR DUNNY
DOOR DOWN

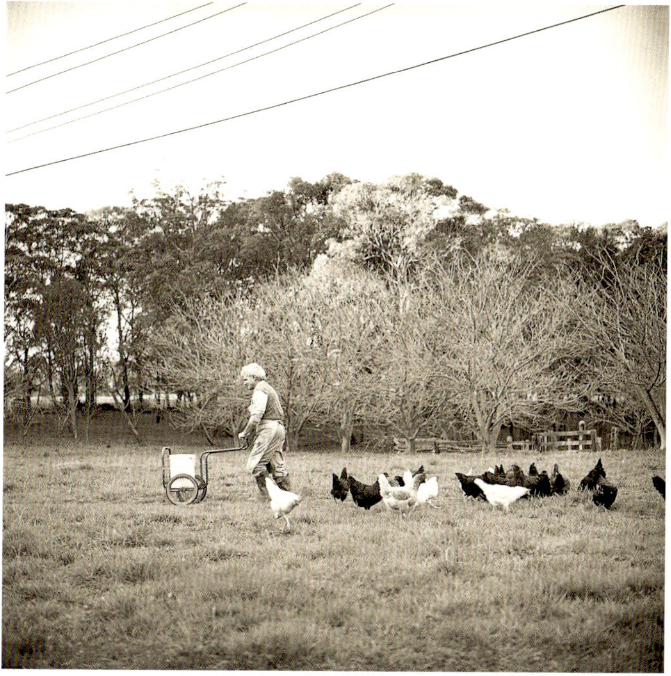

Benedictine Monastery

DRUNK AS A SKUNK **AWAY WITH THE BIRDS** PISSED AS A PARROT **HAVE A HAIR OF THE DOG** MOUTH WILL FEEL LIKE THE BOTTOM OF A COCKY'S CAGE **MY CHOOKS TURNED INTO ROOSTERS AND KICK THE CHOOK HOUSE DOWN** FLY IN THE OINTMENT **RUN AROUND LIKE A BLUE ARSED FLY** WITH IN A BULL'S ROAR **STARVE THE LIZARDS** LIKE A BULL AT A GATE **COCK AND BULL** SOMETHING THE CAT DRAGGED IN **DONE LIKE A DOG'S DINNER** DEAD AS A DODO **STONE THE CROWS** KNEE HIGH TO A GRASSHOPPER **AS DRY AS A DEAD DINGO'S DONGER** GALAH (FOOL) **NERVOUS AS A MOTHER ROO IN A ROOM FULL OF PICKPOCKETS**

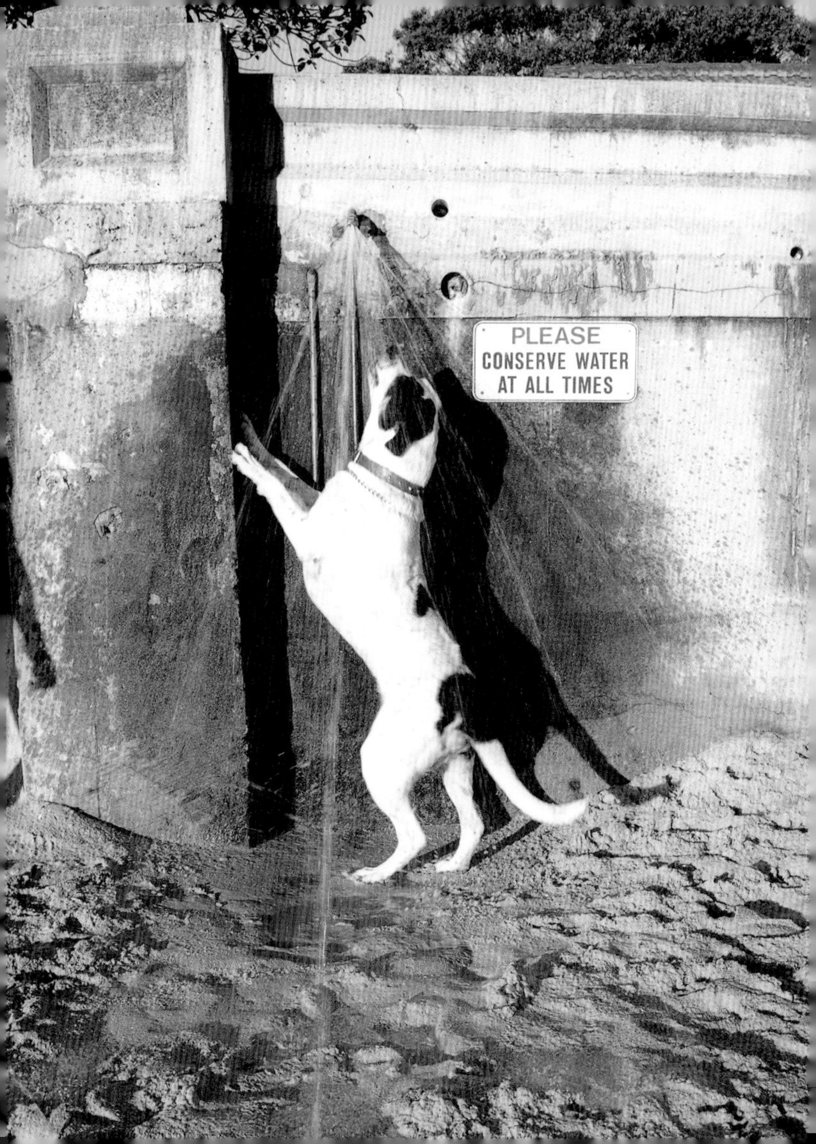
PLEASE
CONSERVE WATER
AT ALL TIMES

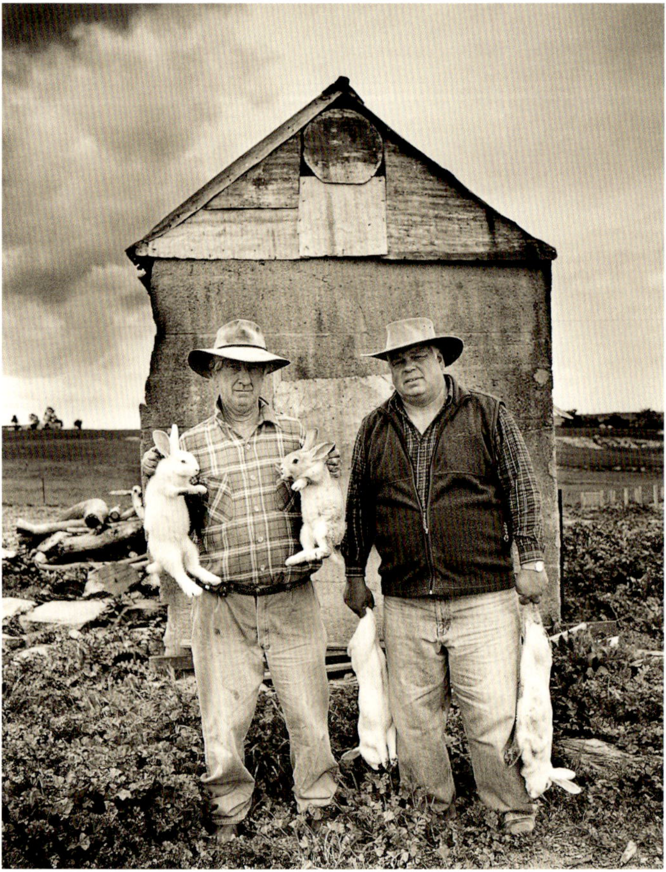

BUNNY BUSINESS
The rabbit farmers of Harden

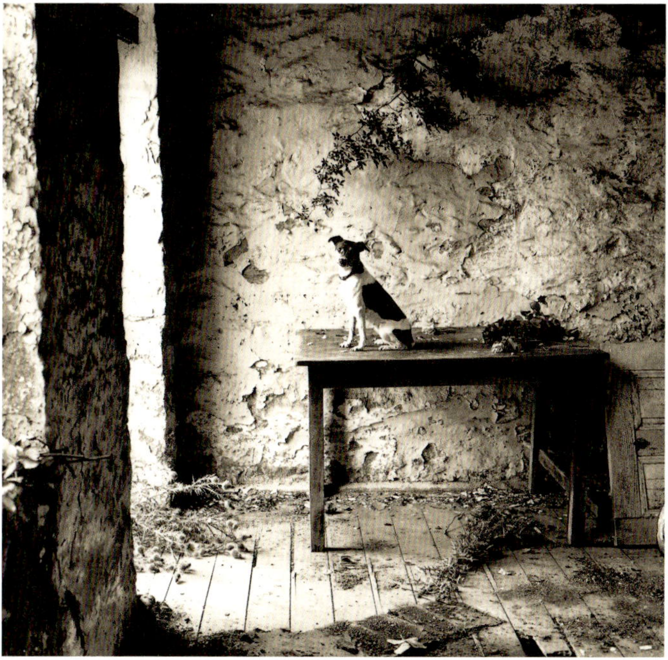

TABLE MANNERS

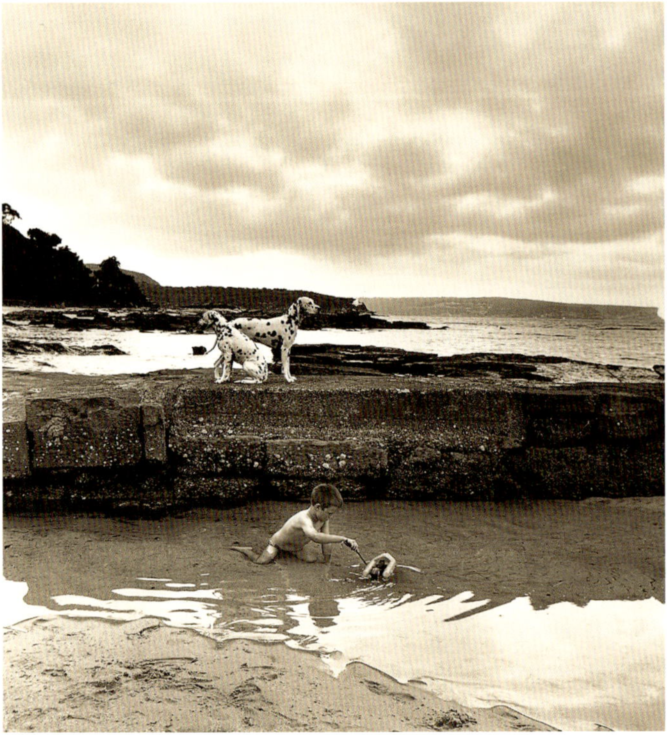

DOG SPOTTING
Balmoral

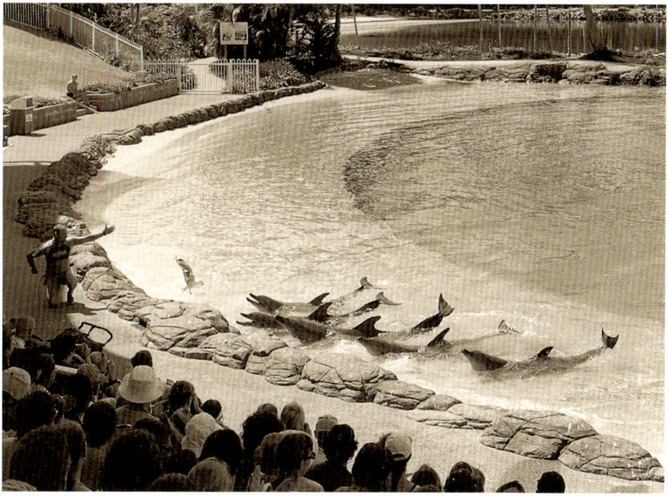

A GATHERING OF DOLPHINS IS CALLED
... IS IT A POD?
Seaworld, Gold Coast

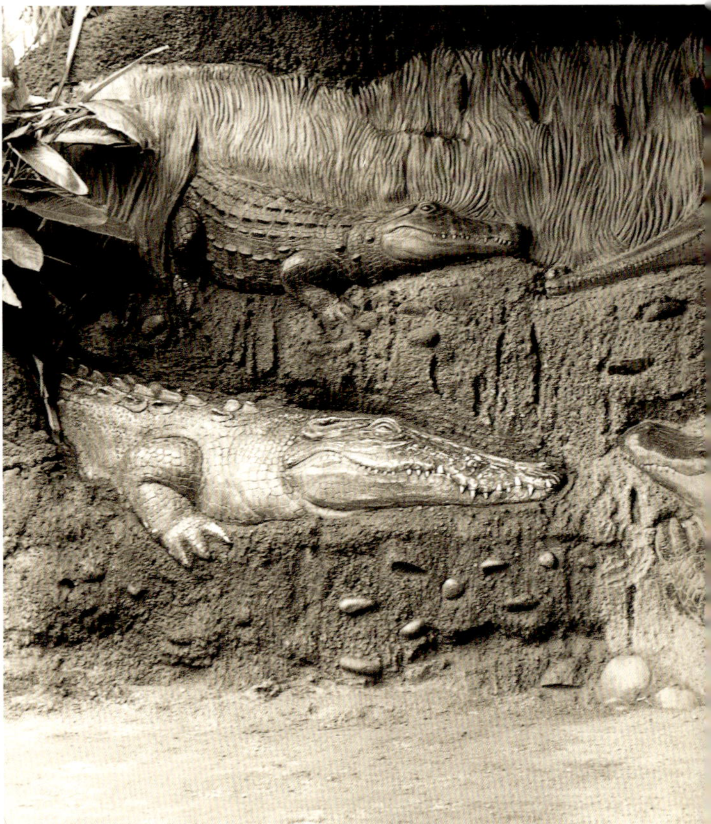

TARONGA ZOO
Sydney

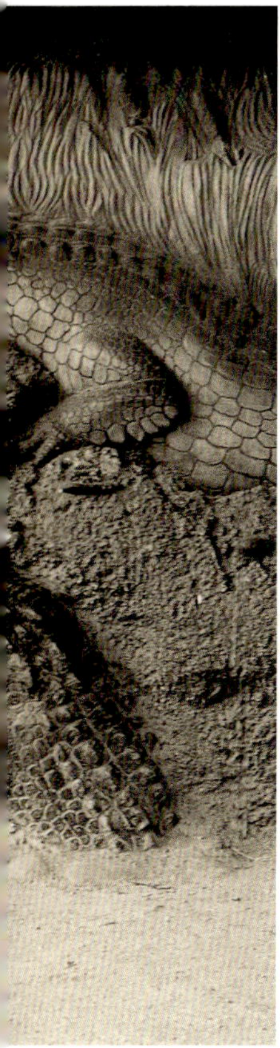

Can I have a
crocodile sandwich
and make it
snappy.

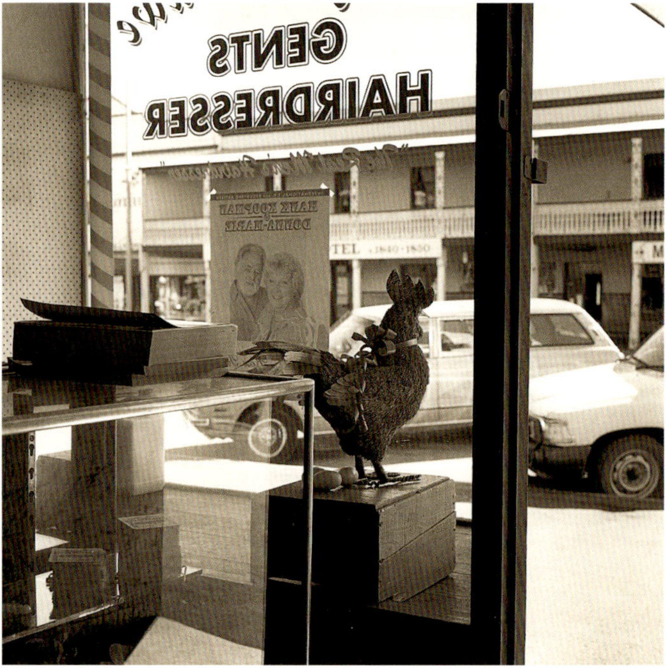

THE ROOSTER WITH THE GOLDEN EGGS
Yass

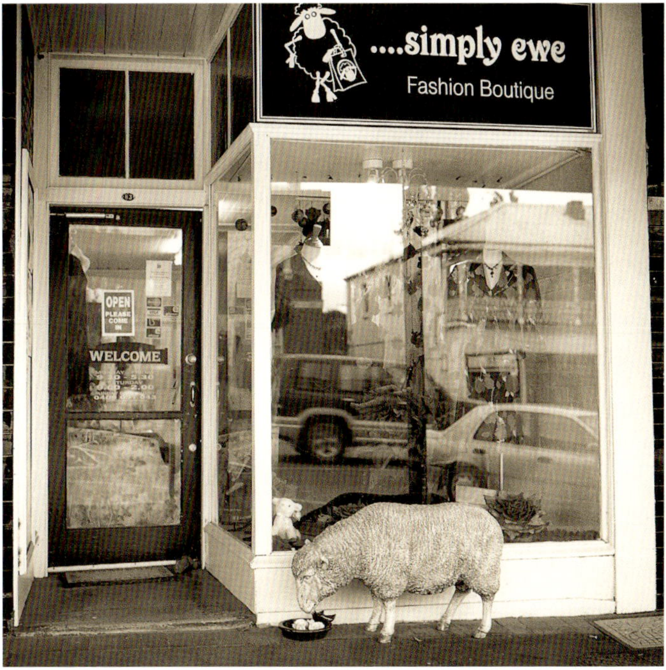

SHEEP EATS

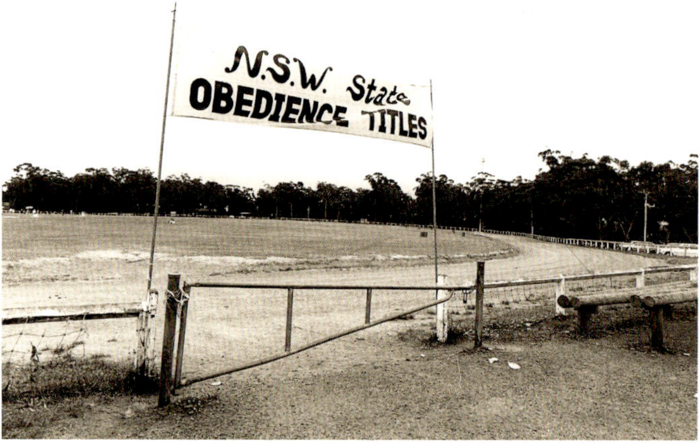

St Ives

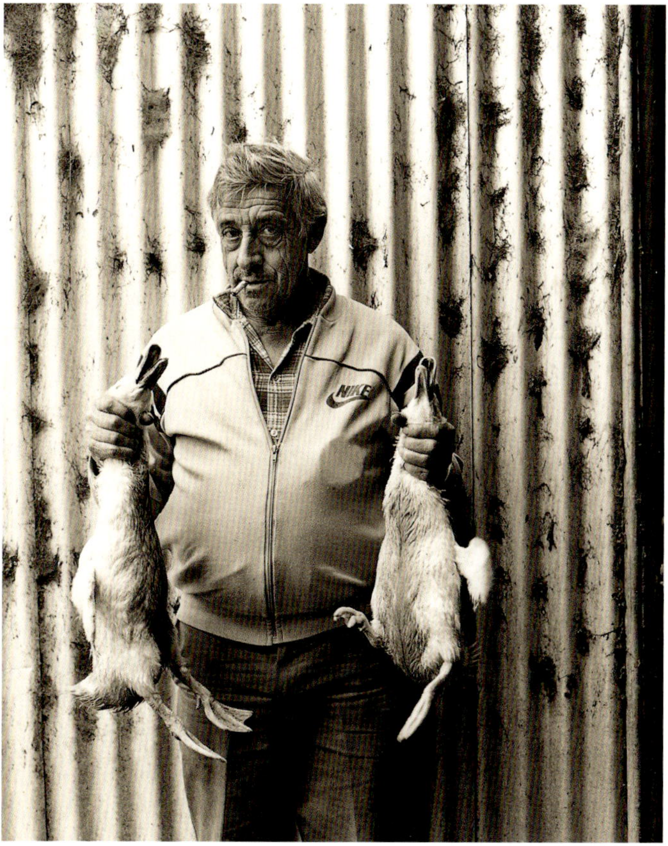

TWO BIRDS IN THE HAND ...
Arcadia

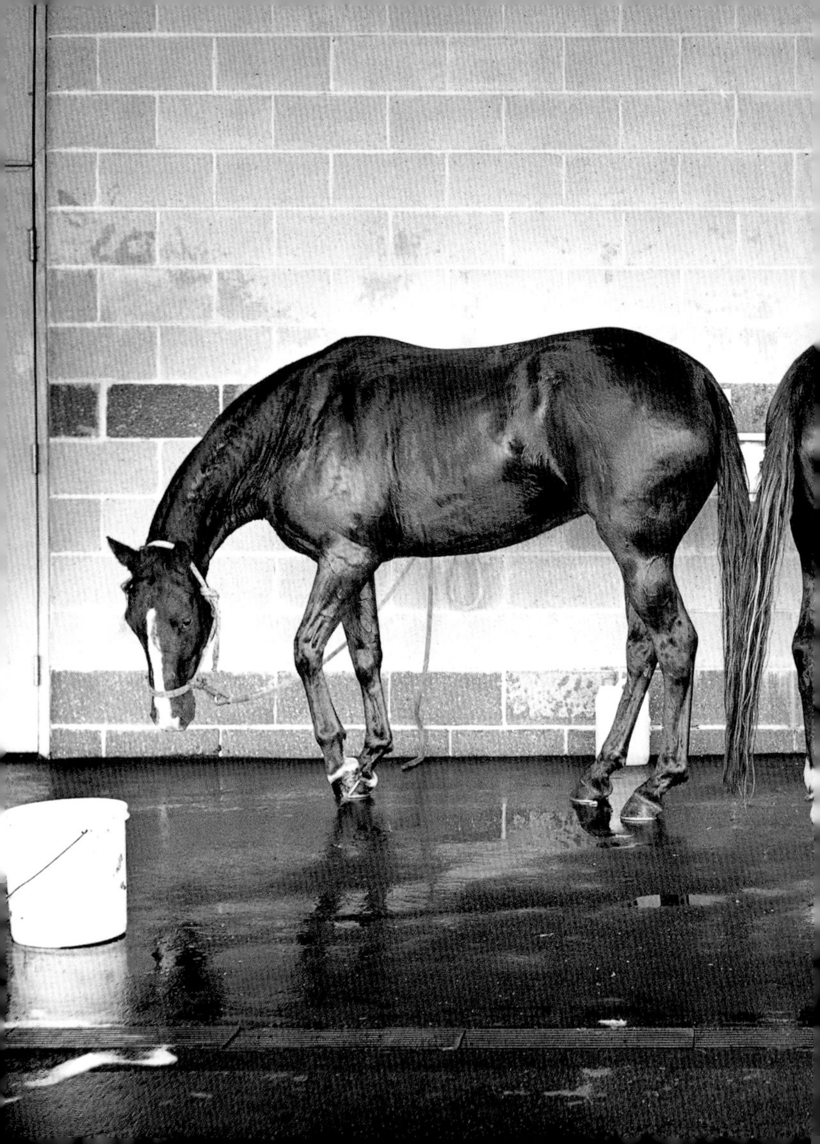

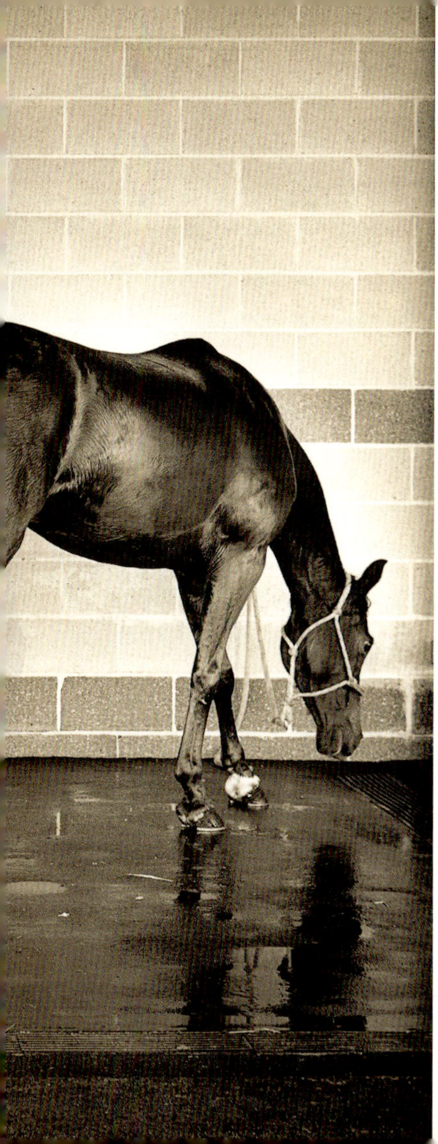

EASTER SHOW
Homebush

Overleaf:
Braidwood, NSW

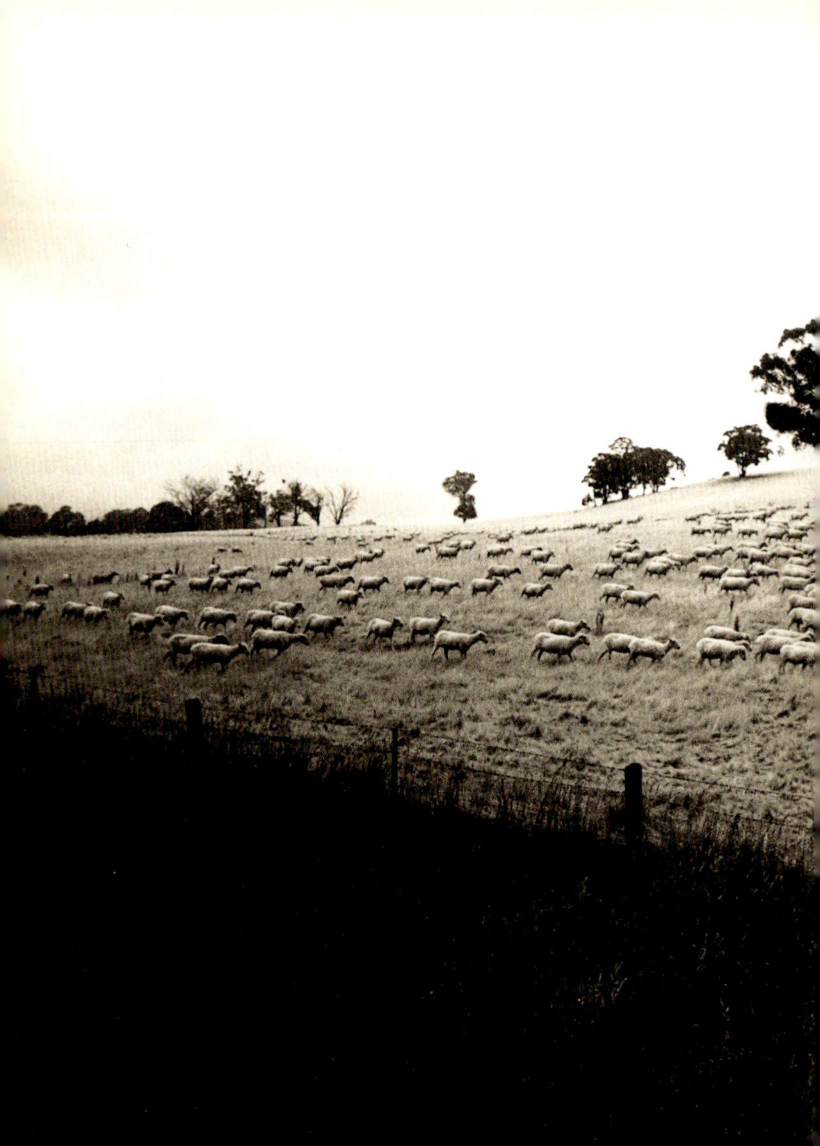

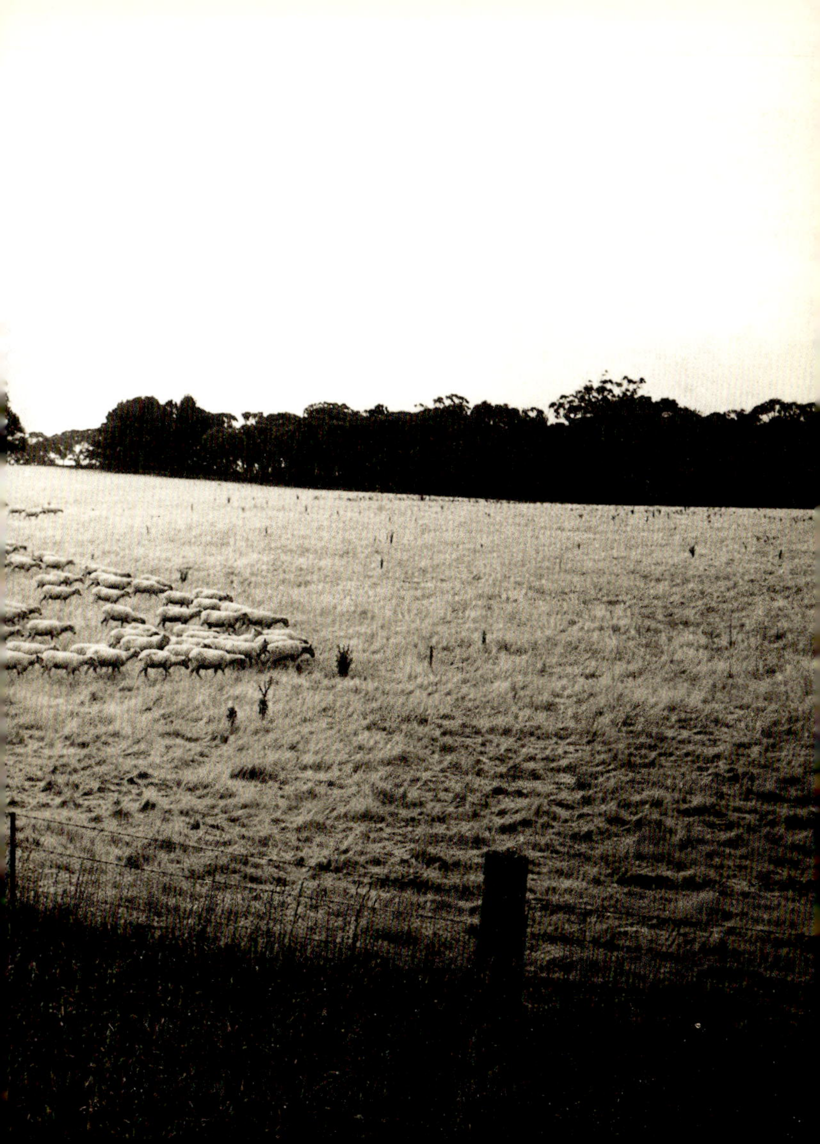

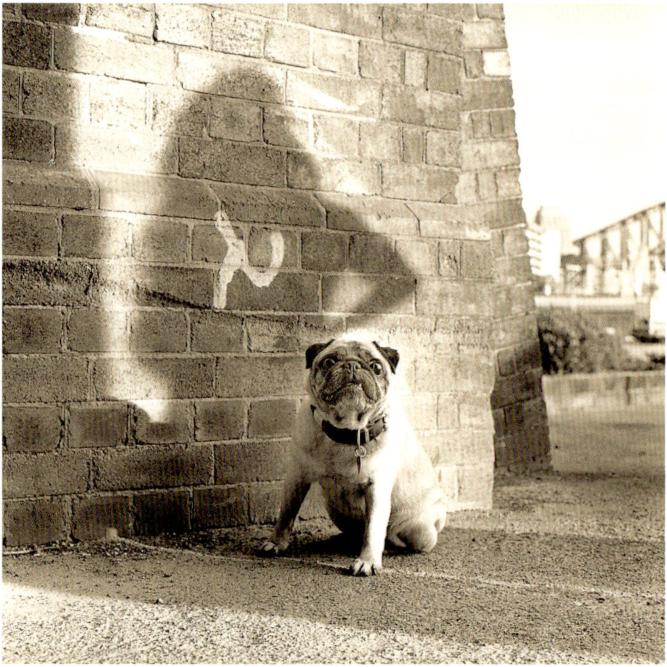

THE SITTING MEMBER
Lavender Bay

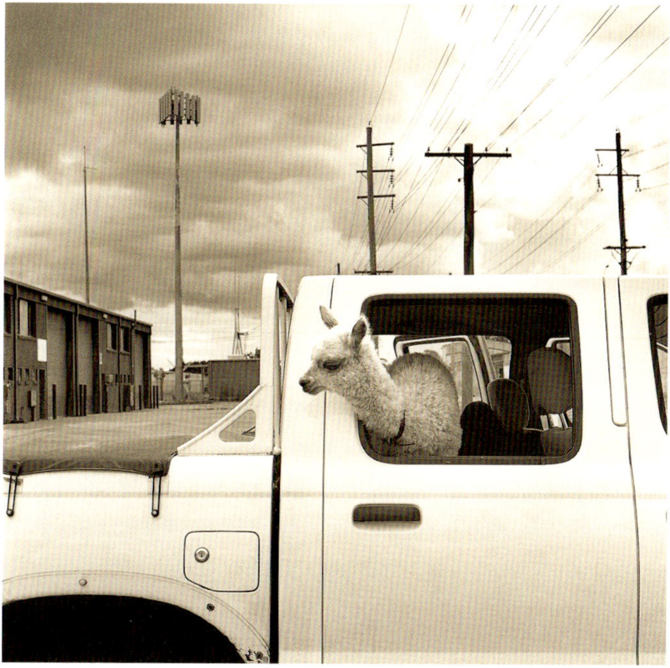

ALPACA ASSISTED PARKING
Liverpool

DOG'S BREAKFAST:
A pee and a trot
around the yard.

CAMOUFLAGE DOG

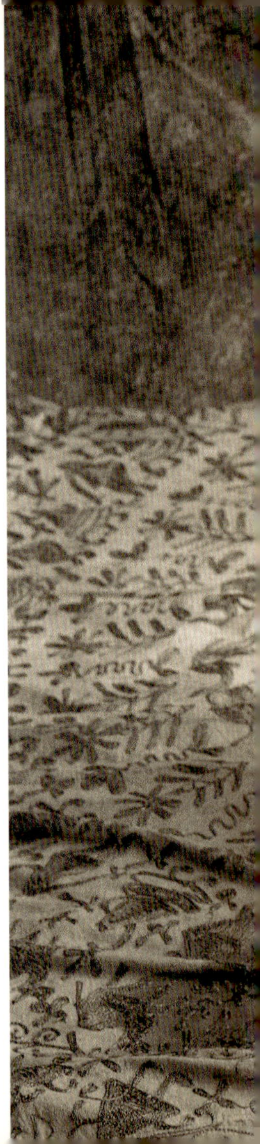

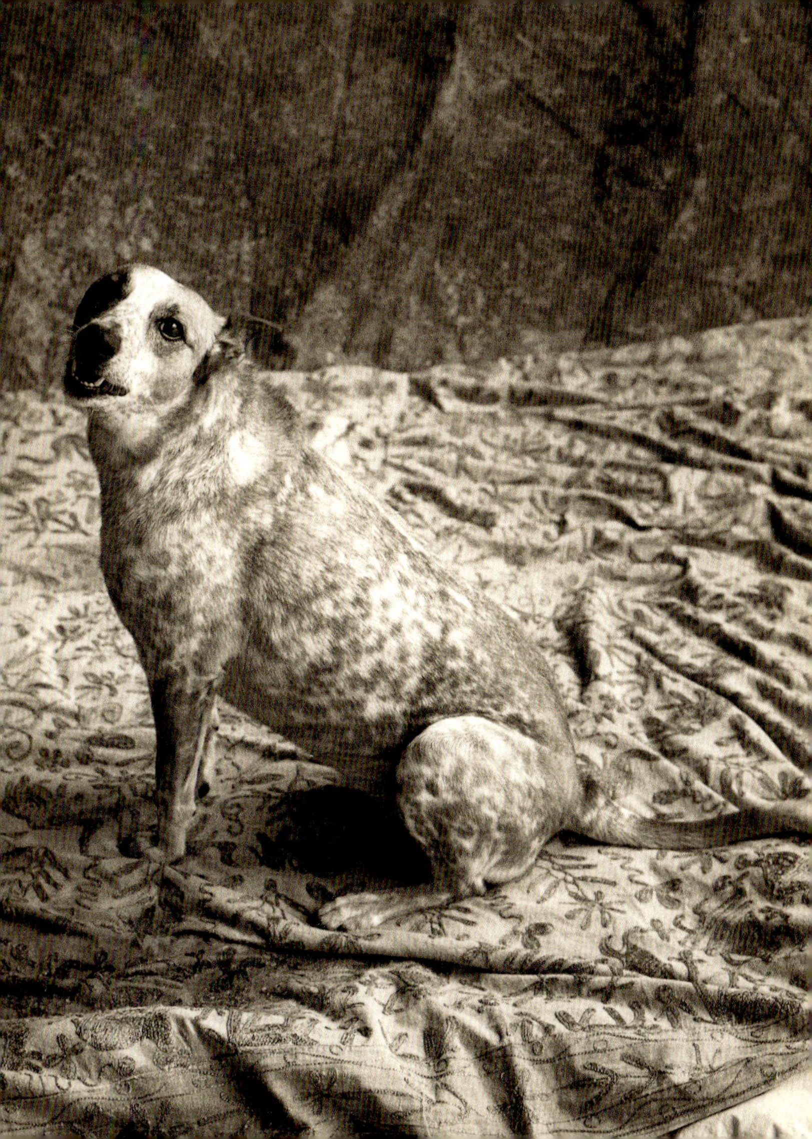

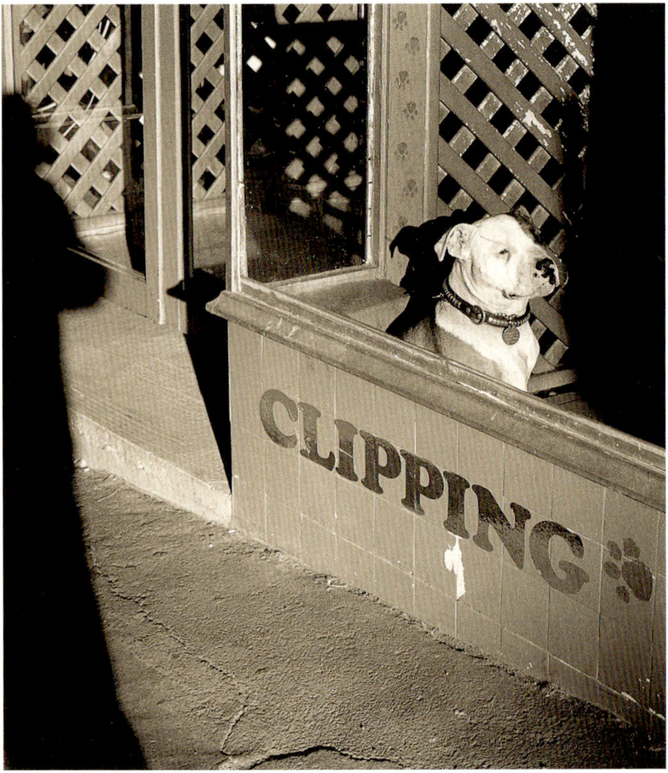

HOW MUCH IS THAT DOGGIE
IN THE WINDOW
Annandale

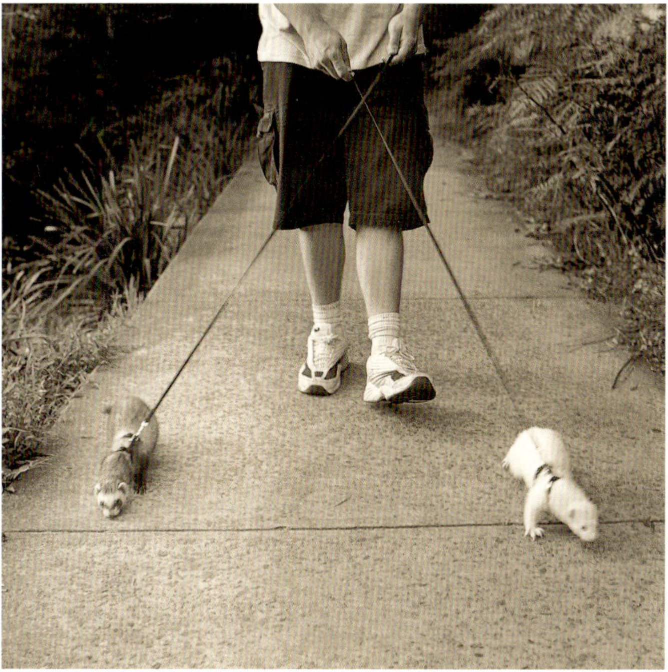

FERRETING AROUND

Overleaf:
SWAN LAKE, Centennial Park

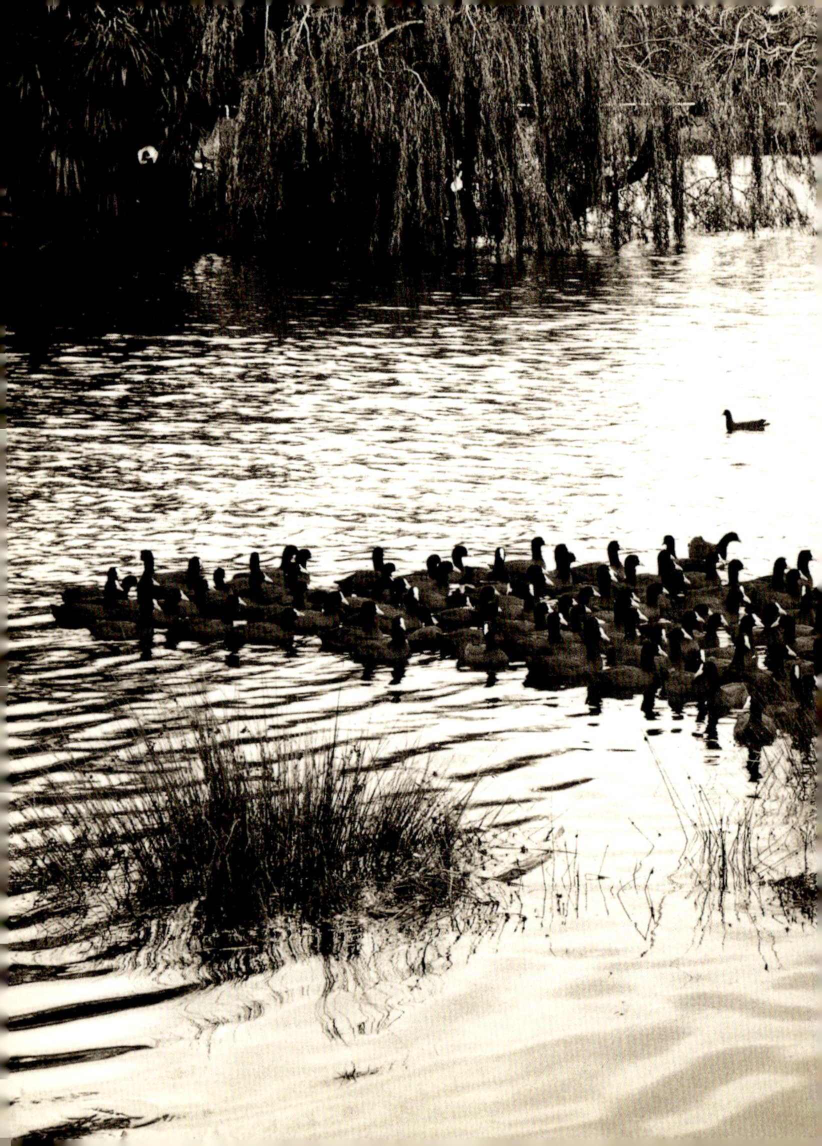

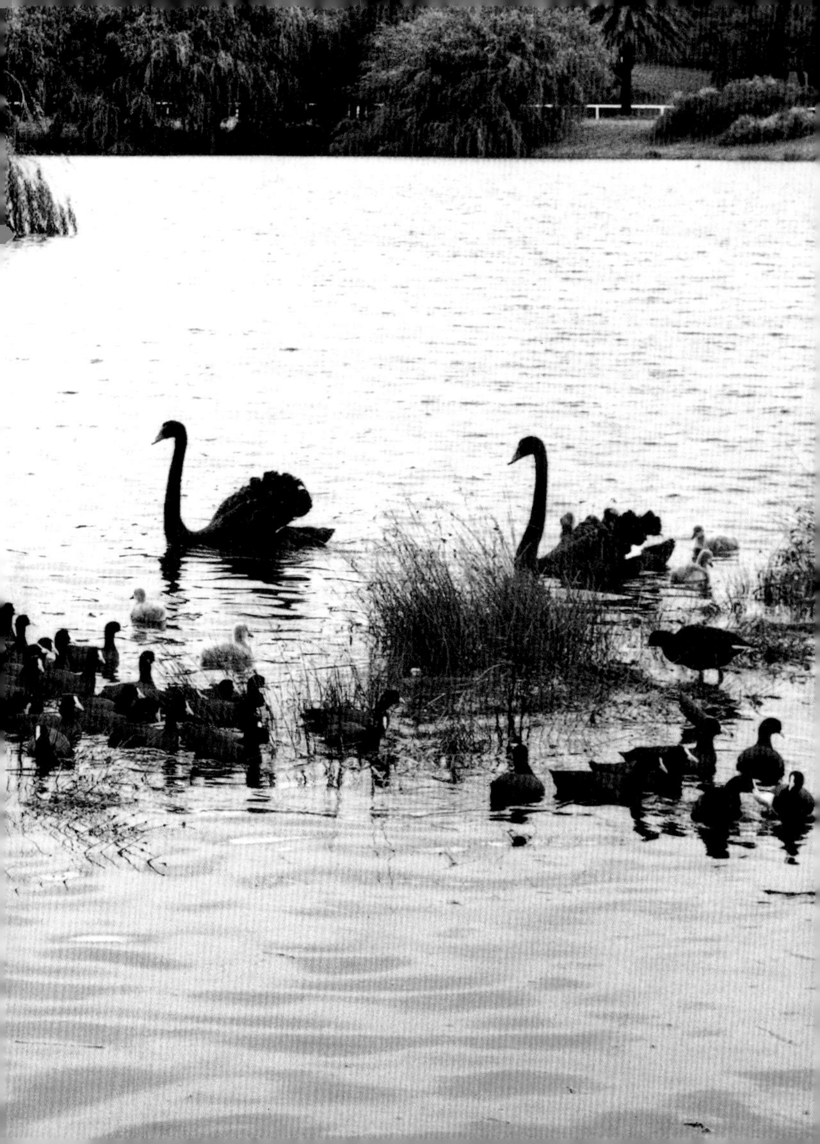

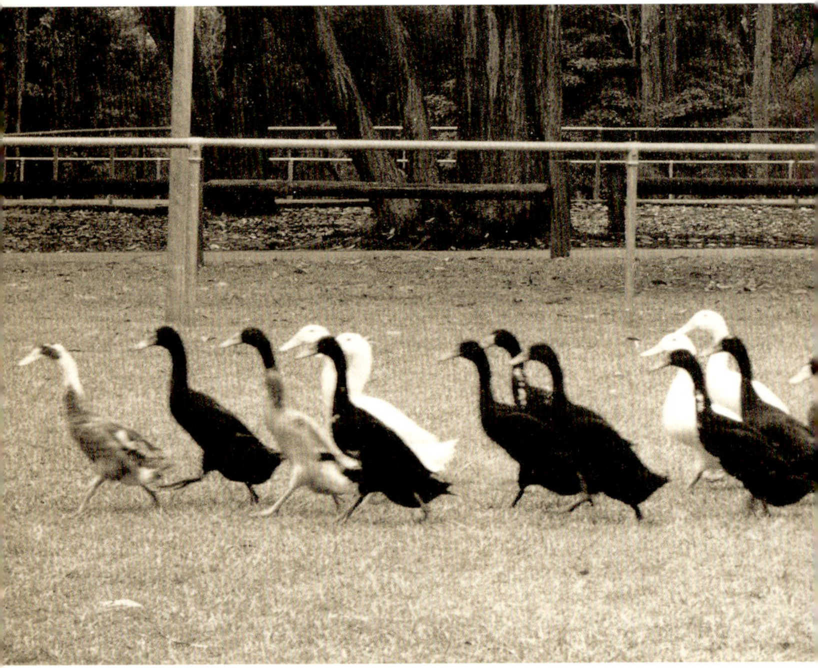

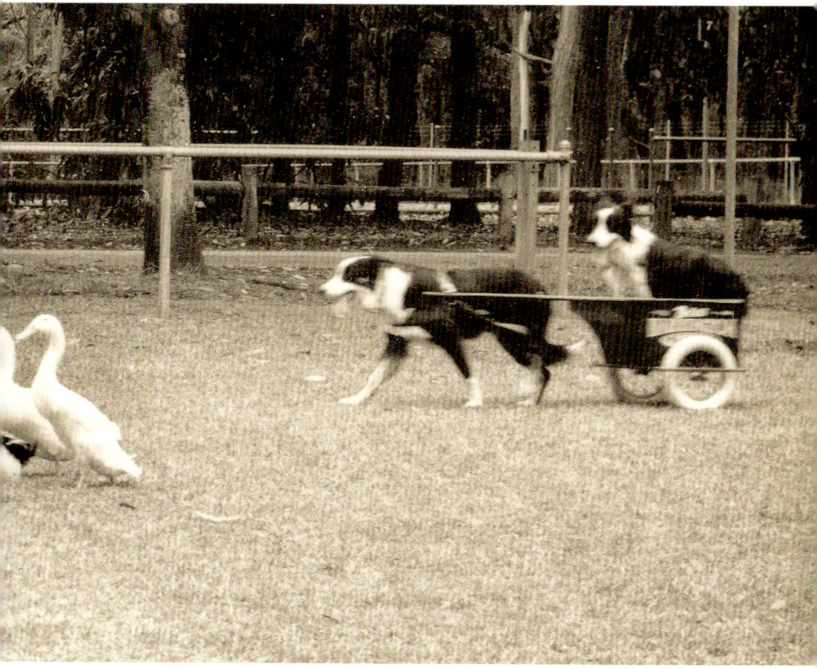

THE AUSTRALIAN ART OF DUCK HERDING

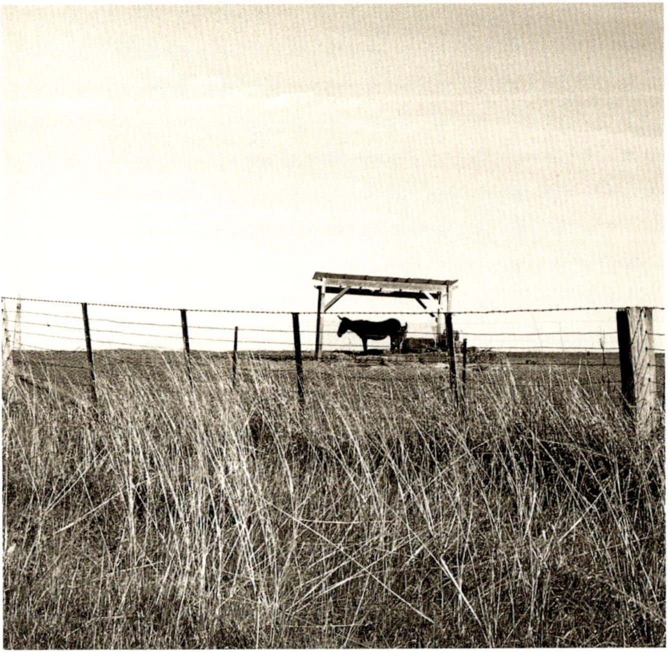

HAVEN'T SEEN HIM IN
DONKEY'S YEARS

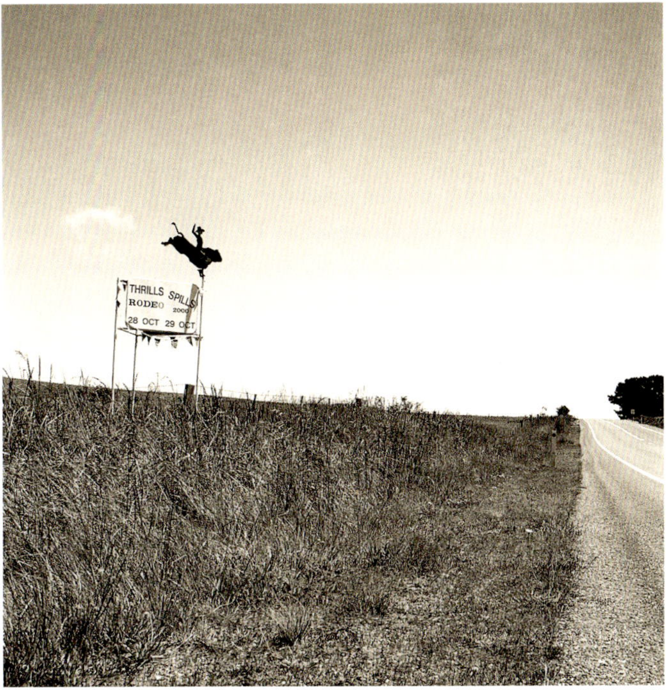

SO HUNGRY I COULD EAT THE HORSE
AND CHASE THE RIDER

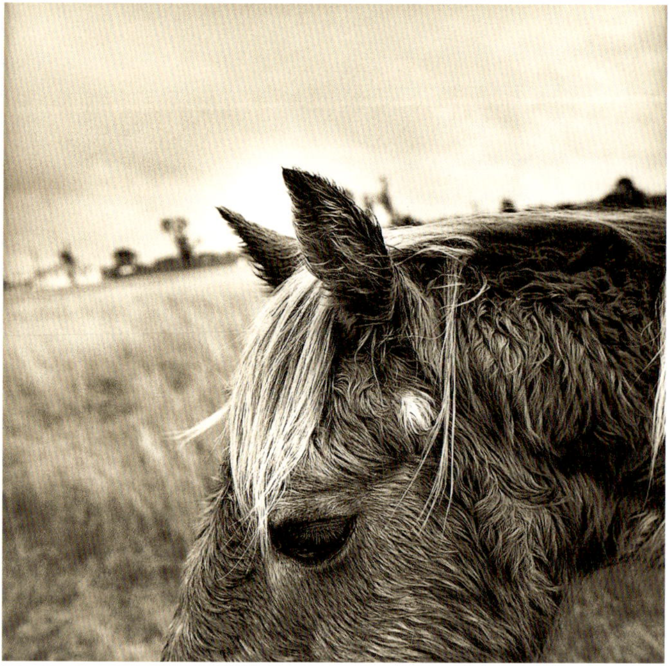

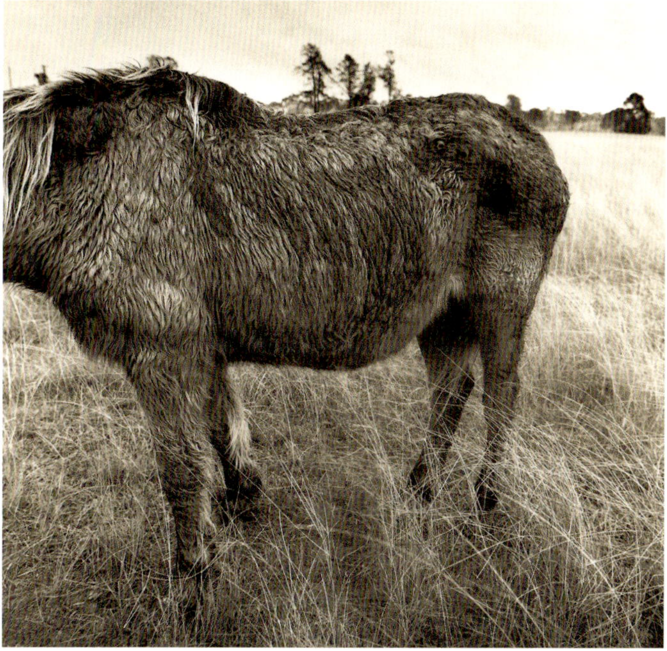

YOU CAN'T KEEP A HORSE IN THE CITY

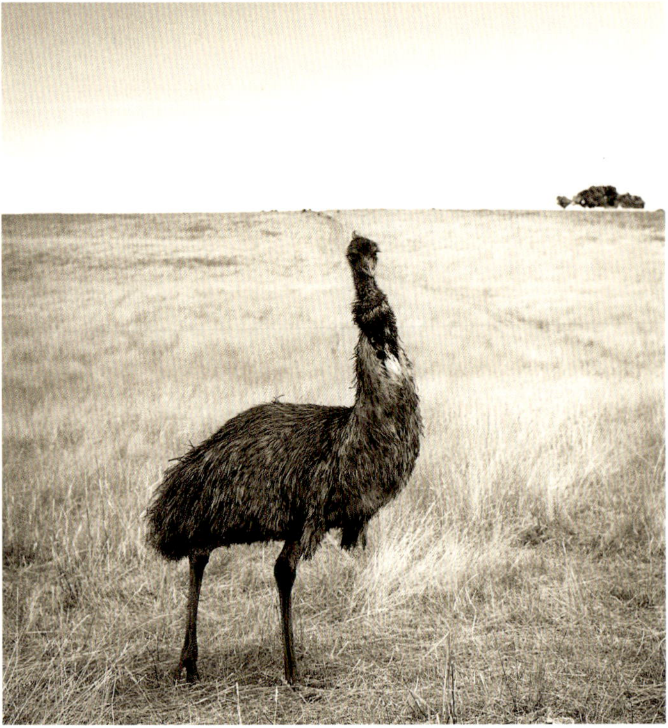

ELLIE THE EMU

The emu brought up as an Alpaca, Yass

ACKNOWLEDGMENTS

To all the owners and minders of the animals who agreed to pose for me. Dennis and Brenda Hare who inspired the Australianisms and prompted opportunities. The Billington kids and their pets and my wife Julianne.

First published in 2004 by WriteLight Pty Ltd for
Sparklehorse Publishing
7a Clarke Street, Crows Nest NSW 2065, Australia
Ph: 61 2 9901 4440, Fax: 61 2 9439 1989
www.billingtonphotography.com.au

ISBN 09581934 6 0

Design: Julianne Billington
Production: Victoria Jefferys
Produced in Hong Kong by Phoenix Offset

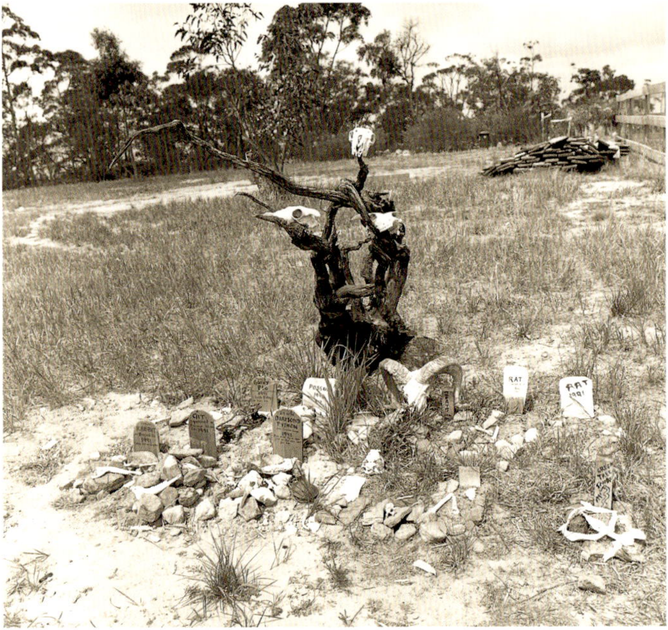

REST CAMP (CEMETERY)

O TIE UP A DOG (GET DRINKS ON CREDIT)

INNER **AWAY WITH THE BIRDS** PISSED AS A

EEL LIKE THE BOTTOM OF A COCKY'S CAGE

HE CHOOK HOUSE DOWN FLY IN THE OI

ITHIN A BULL'S ROAR **STARVE THE LIZA**

OMETHING THE CAT DRAGGED IN **SEE A MA**

ROWS KNEE HIGH TO A GRASSHOPPER **JUST**

ROOM FULL OF PICKPOCKETS **I COULD EAT**

AMEL DRIVER'S BUM **GALAH (FOOL)** TO TIE

RUNK (DRUNK) DONE LIKE A DOGS DINN

HAVE A HAIR OF THE DOG MOUTH WILL

HOOKS TURNED INTO ROOSTERS AND

INTMENT **RUN AROUND LIKE A BLUE A**

IZARDS LIKE A BULL AT A GATE **COCK AND**

BOUT A DOG DEAD AS A DODO **STONE THE**

EES KNEES NERVOUS AS A MOTHER ROO I

HORSE AND CHASE THE RIDER I'M AS DRY A

A DOG (GET DRINKS ON CREDIT) **ELEPHAN**

AWAY WITH THE BIRDS PISSED AS